The vocacyon
of Johan Bale

medieval & renaissance texts & studies

VOLUME 70

RENAISSANCE ENGLISH TEXT SOCIETY

SEVENTH SERIES

VOL. XIV (1989)

The vocacyon
of Johan Bale

edited by

PETER HAPPÉ AND JOHN N. KING

medieval & renaissance texts & studies
in conjunction with
Renaissance English Text Society
Binghamton, New York
1990

Library of Congress Cataloging-in-Publication Data

Bale, John, 1495–1563.
    The vocacyon of Johan Bale / edited by Peter
Happé and John N. King.
        p. cm.—(Medieval & Renaissance texts &
studies ; v. 70)
    Includes bibliographical references.
    ISBN 0-86698-079-2
    1. Bale, John, 1495–1563.   2. Church of Ireland—
Bishops—Biography.   3.Anglican Communion—
Ireland—Bishops—Biography—Early works to 1800.
    I. Happé, Peter, 1932-   II. King, John N., 1945- .
III. Title.   IV Series.
BX5595.B3B35   1990
283'.092—dc20
[B]   89–38379
                                                         CIP

This book is made to last.
It is set in Trump, smythe-sewn,
and printed on acid-free paper
to library specifications.

Printed in the United States of America

Contents

Illustrations

Acknowledgements

The editors wish to thank the Librarian of the Cambridge University Library for granting permission to print from the copy text, and for supplying xeroxes and photographs. Gordon Kipling has played an instrumental role by introducing us and encouraging the project. Richard and Marie Axton have kindly allowed us to follow in the Notes certain printing conventions used in their Tudor Interludes series. Dr. Luther Waddington King has helped with checking the text and preparing the Index of Biblical Texts.

We should also like to acknowledge much helpful support from staff at the following: the British Library (especially David Paisey), the Bodleian Library, Columbia University Library, the Folger Shakespeare Library (especially Nati Kravitsky), the Houghton Library at Harvard University, the Ladd Library of Bates College (especially Thomas Hayward), Lambeth Palace Library, Lincoln Cathedral and Nottingham University Libraries, the Library of Trinity College, Cambridge, and of the Queen's University of Belfast, and the Southampton and York University Libraries.

Abbreviations

Answer
The answer of John Bale pryst unto serten artycles (1537), MS PRO SP 1/111, fols. 183–87.

Apology
The Apology of Johan Bale agaynste a ranke Papyst (London: S. Mierdman, 1550), STC 1275.

Bagwell
Richard Bagwell, *Ireland under the Tudors*, 3 vols. (London: Green & Co., 1885–90).

BCP 1
The Booke of the Common Prayer and Administration of the Sacramentes, and Other Rites and Ceremonies of the Churche (1549). See *The First Prayer-Book of Edward VI Compared with Successive Revisions of The Book of Common Prayer* (Oxford and London: James Parker & Co., 1877).

BCP 2
Second version (1552).

Book of Homilies
Certayne Sermons, or Homilies (Worcester: John Oswen, 1549), STC 13645.

"Books and Manuscripts"
H. C. McCusker, "Books and MSS formerly in the Possession of John Bale," *The Library*, Fourth Series, 16 (1936): 144–65.

Bradshaw
Brendan Bradshaw, "The Edwardian Reformation in Ireland, 1547–53," *Archivium Hibernicum* 34 (1976): 83–99.

Catalogus
John Bale, *Scriptorum Illustrium maioris Britanniae . . . Catalogus*, 2 vols. (Basel: J. Oporinus, 1557–59).

Complete Plays	Peter Happé, ed., *The Complete Plays of John Bale*, 2 vols. (Cambridge: Boydell and Brewer, 1985–86).
Davies	W. T. Davies, "A Bibliography of John Bale," *Oxford Bibliographical Society, Proceedings and Papers* 5 (1940): 203–79.
EA	Indicates possible East Anglian dialect form.
Edwards	R. Dudley Edwards, *Church and State in Tudor Ireland* (London: Longmans Green & Co., 1935).
ERL	John N. King, *English Reformation Literature: The Tudor Origins of the Protestant Tradition* (Princeton: Princeton Univ. Press, 1982).
FQ	Edmund Spenser, *The Faerie Queene*, ed. A. C. Hamilton (London and New York, 1977).
GP	John Bale, *A Tragedye or enterlude manyfestyng the chefe promyses of God* (Wesel: Dirik van der Straten, 1547), STC 1305, in *Complete Plays*.
History	Geoffrey of Monmouth, *Historia Regum Britanniae* (1136); trans. Lewis Thorpe, *The History of the Kings of Britain* (Harmondsworth: Penguin Books, 1966).
Image	John Bale, *The Image of both Churches* (Antwerp: S. Mierdman, 1545), STC 1296.5.
Injunctions	*Injunccions geven by the moste excellent prince Edward the sixte* (London: R. Grafton, 1547).
JBP	John Bale, *John Baptystes Preachynge* (1547), in *Complete Plays*.
KJ	John Bale, *King Johan* (?1538–1559), in *Complete Plays*.
Laws	John Bale, *A Comedy concernynge thre lawes of nature, Moses and Christ* (Wesel: Dirik van der Straten, 1548), STC 1287, in *Complete Plays*.
OED	J. A. H. Murray *et al.*, eds., *The Oxford English Dictionary*, 13 vols. (Oxford, 1933).
PL	John Milton, *Paradise Lost*, in *Complete Poems and Major Prose*, ed. Merritt Y. Hughes (New York: Odyssey Press, 1957).
PrP	A. L. Mayhew, ed., *Promptorium Parvulorum*, EETS, e.s. 102 (London: Oxford Univ. Press, 1908).
STC	*A Short Title Catalogue of Books Printed in England, Scotland and Ireland 1475–1640*, ed. A. W. Pollard and G. R. Redgrave (1926); 2nd edition revised and enlarged by W. A. Jackson, F. S. Ferguson, K. F. Panzer, 2 vols. (London: The Bibliographical Society, 1976 and 1986).
Summarium	John Bale, *Illustrium maioris Britanniae scriptorum Summarium* (Wesel: Dirik van der Straten, 1548), STC 1295.

Temptation	*A brefe Comedy or enterlude concernynge the temp-tacyon of oure lorde and saver Jesus Christ* (Wesel: Dirik van der Straten, 1547), STC 1279, in *Complete Plays.*
Tilley	M. P. Tilley, *A Dictionary of the Proverbs in England in the Sixteenth and Seventeenth Centuries* (Ann Arbor: Univ. of Michigan Press, 1950).
Votaryes	John Bale, *The Actes of Englysh Votaryes* (Antwerp: S. Mierdman, 1546), STC 1270.
vulg.	*Biblia Sacra* (Madrid: Biblioteca de Autores Cristianos, 1977).
Whiting	B. J. and H. W. Whiting, *Proverbs, Sentences, and Proverbial Phrases* (Cambridge, Mass.: Harvard Univ. Press, 1968).
†	Used in Glossary and Notes to indicate that this is the first *OED* reference or predates it.

Introduction

As a member of the first generation of English Protestants, John Bale played an active role in the Tudor Reformation from the time of his conversion under the impetus of Tyndale's ideas until the 1559 settlement of religion. In his career as a religious reformer he experienced sharply contrasting intervals of success and adversity during the reigns of four Tudor sovereigns. Despite an initial period of favor under the Cromwell regime, Bale went into exile during the religious reaction of Henry VIII's last decade. After his return under the more radically Protestant government of Edward VI, royal patronage led him to embark upon a brief career as a missionary bishop in Ireland. The young king's early death and the religious reversal under his Catholic successor, Mary I, precipitated yet another flight to seek safe haven in foreign exile. Having returned soon after the accession of Elizabeth I, Bale lived out his remaining years in England. During his long career as an ecclesiastical reformer, he demonstrated varied capabilities as a prolific author, editor, preacher, dramatist, controversialist, antiquary, scholar, collector of books and manuscripts, bibliographer, historian, biblical commentator, and evangelical bishop. The stridency with which he discharged his episcopal duties at a see in an outlying region of the royal dominions provided the occasion for the creation of *The vocacyon of Johan Bale to the bishoprick of Ossorie in Irelande his persecucions in the same / and finall delyveraunce* (1553). Bale wrote this colorful account of his appointment and brief tenure as a missionary bishop at the outset of his second flight into exile on the Continent.

Life and Works

Despite Bale's distant wandering from the place of his birth near the coastal town of Dunwich in Suffolk on 21 November 1495, he continued to assert not only his nationality as an Englishman but also a provincial identity as a Suffolkman.[1] He entered the house of the Carmelite friars in Norwich as a twelve-year-old before going up to Cambridge in 1514. Long-standing tradition holds that he went to Jesus College, where he came into contact with Thomas Cranmer, who was then a Fellow.[2] His conventional scholarly interests as a member of the Carmelite order demonstrated little, if any, impact of new humanistic learning or the Lutheran ideas that were taking root at Cambridge during the 1520s when Cranmer, Latimer, Coverdale, and others met for regular discussion at the White Horse tavern. Although surviving records indicate only that Bale received his B.D. in 1529, the university presumably granted him the B.A. and M.A., and ultimately the D.D. as well. After visits to the Low Countries and France, he returned to East Anglia to serve as the prior of Carmelite houses, first in Maldon and then at Ipswich. His writings contain many East Anglian dialect usages.

Bale's conversion to Protestantism, which took place later than those of many other early reformers, probably occurred in 1534. According to his own account, he converted under the influence of Thomas, first Baron Wentworth, whose manor at Nettlestead was immediately northwest of Ipswich. As an important East Anglian peer, Wentworth was an influential courtier and prominent patron of Protestant learning. He had fallen under the influence of the Lutheran ideas that Tyndale, Latimer, and others domesticated. Bale became Wentworth's protégé after moving to Ipswich to head the Carmelite house in that city.[3] His conversion must have been complete by the time that he left the religious order in 1536, while the Dissolution of the Lesser Monasteries was in progress, because he married and assumed parochial duties as a secular priest in Thorndon, a village in Suffolk. He was in a difficult position as a preacher because of the conservatism of the Reformation under Henry VIII, whose replacement of the pope as the supreme head of the church left traditional theology and ritual intact. Bale's imprisonment for heresy in the following year elicited an admission that he questioned doctrine and ritual lacking a basis in the scriptures.[4] The intercession of Bale's colleague John Leland, the King's Antiquary, led to his release through the intervention of Thomas Cromwell. As Leland's collaborator, Bale had already undertaken the labor that would occupy him for the rest of his life, the recording of all writings in manuscript and print by British authors. In order to prevent the loss of learning because of the destruction of monastic libraries, they undertook the monumental bibliographical project that resulted in the publication of Bale's *Summarium* and *Catalogus*.

Bale acknowledges that Cromwell obtained his release "on account of comedies he had written" ("ob editas comoedias").[5] As the king's chief minister and vicegerent in religious affairs, Cromwell patronized a group of Protestant publicists who wrote in favor of the royal supremacy, the disestablishment of the monasteries, and the campaign against pilgrimages and religious images. (These propagandists included Thomas Starkey, Richard Moryson, and William Marshall.) At about the time that Cromwell collaborated with Thomas Cranmer, Archbishop of Canterbury, to secure the landmark publication of the Great Bible (1539) — the first authorized English translation of the scriptures — Bale was actively involved in the writing and production of polemical plays that violently attacked the pope as Antichrist and the entire Roman church establishment. Cromwell underwrote the group of players who performed the plays. The most innovative and complicated of these dramatic works to have survived is *King Johan*, a morality play that flatters Henry VIII as a reforming monarch at the same time that it encourages him to undertake a more thorough-going Protestant program. Cranmer offered a venue for performing *King Johan* in his household during Christmastide 1538–39.[6]

Even before Cromwell's fall, the passage of the Act of Six Articles (1539) marked the onset of a major policy shift in the direction of religious reaction, reimposition of strict orthodoxy, and persecution of heretics. The minister's execution in the following year provided Bale's signal to flee into Continental exile with his wife and family. During the next eight years he composed anti-Catholic tracts that attacked the papacy for distorting "pure" religion by imposing excess ritualism, superstitious devotion to the cults of saints and the Virgin Mary, and belief in transubstantiation and the mass as a continuing sacrifice. He contended that the Protestant practices that he advocated in their place would nurture individual faith by means of gospel preaching, lay education in the vernacular Bible, and a communion service that commemorates the remembrance of Christ's sacrifice as the sole means of salvation. These works were published in Antwerp until the suppression of Protestant printing in that city, and then in Wesel, a center of publication immediately beyond Hapsburg control, which maintained easy shipping connections down the Rhine and across the North Sea to Ipswich and other English ports.

Chief in importance among the works of Bale's first exile is the *Image of Both Churches* (Antwerp, c. 1545–48), the first full-length Protestant commentary on Revelation published in English. It outlines an apocalyptic theory of history as an ongoing conflict between the "true" church, which has maintained faith and worship based upon the gospels ever since the apostolic age, and the "false" church, which, according to Bale, was subverted by Antichrist in 607 when Pope Boniface III obtained recognition from Emperor Phocas as head of the church of Rome.[7] This dualistic pattern has informed the historical ages prophesied by the opening of the seven seals and blowing of the seven trumpets until the triumph of Antichrist during the sixth age, when nonscriptural traditions like clerical celibacy and the worship of religious images were introduced. Bale identifies the sixth epoch with the persecution of Wyclif and Huss during the fourteenth and fifteenth centuries.[8] This age has endured until the present moment, in Bale's view, when the Reformation controversy anticipates the victory of truth and the imminent end of the world (see note on ll. 567–77). The monastic orders that Bale implicates in the temporary defeat of the "true" church during the sixth age also come under attack in *The Actes of Englysh Votaryes* (Antwerp, 1546) by means of lurid charges of sexual license, depravity, and homosexuality within the religious houses. Of particular interest are two efforts at recasting the medieval genre of the saint's life, which Bale attacks for supplanting the scriptures in popular devotion with tales of "false" miracles and superstitious practices. His accounts of the martyrdom of Sir John Oldcastle and Anne Askew redefine sainthood along the lines of the Protestant doctrine of the sainthood of all believers.[9] Bale joins the attack against the Catholic separation of the laity from both saints and clergy, to whom are attributed the supernatural powers of working miracles and interceding for the salvation of souls. Like other reformers, he affirms that sanctification is accessible to any elect Christian who testifies or gives witness to faith in Christ, to the point of death if necessary. Protestant saints are seen to remain faithful to the precepts of the "true" apostolic church.

Unlike the works cited above, Bale's *Summarium* came off the press in Wesel after the death of Henry VIII on 28 January 1547. Dirik van der Straten's printing of the work on 31 July 1548, with variant imprints designed for separate publication in Wesel and Ipswich, gives evidence of the major policy shift that followed the accession of Edward VI as a nine-year-old boy. The lords who governed England during his minority (first Edward Seymour, Protector Somerset, and then John Dudley, Earl of Warwick and later Duke of Northumberland) embraced a thorough-going program of Protestant reforms of the kind that the late king had suppressed during his final years on the throne. One consequence of this change was the repeal of the Act of Six Articles and the existing statutes against heresy, an action which extended unprecedented liberty of speech and publication to members of the Protestant faction. The organization of *Summarium* reflects the change in Bale's fortune and his imminent return to England, because a dedication to Edward VI accompanies the title-page woodcut portraying the author handing a copy of his book to the young king in his presence chamber. This dedication and illustration incorporate a powerful appeal for patronage from the new regime.

The assistance of the Crown was not forthcoming, however, until after the fall of Protector Somerset in 1549, in all likelihood because *The First Examinacyon of Anne Askewe* had attacked Sir William Paget for urging the Protestant martyr to recant prior to her execution (sig. C7^r). Remaining in the office of Principal Secretary after he had assisted Somerset in what was effectively a *coup d'état*, Paget was well placed to block Bale from advancement. Although the author must have seemed like a natural candidate to receive patronage from a staunchly Protestant king, his only support during the early part of the new reign came from the Duchess of Richmond. The Earl of Warwick's seizure of power in 1549 opened the way to Bale's preferment to benefices from the Crown and from John Ponet, Bishop of Winchester, who appointed his friend rector of the Church of St. Mary in Bishopstoke, Hampshire, where he also served in the bishop's manor as a chaplain. Bale received his highest clerical appointment during Edward VI's summer progress of 1552. The account in the *Vocacyon* of Bale's going to see the royal entourage and being recognized in the street when he was thought to be "bothe dead & buried" (ll. 613–14) may contain an ironic aside on his sense of having been passed over for higher office. It is impossible to determine whether his presence was fortuitous, or whether he had been invited by a friend at court. John Philpot arranged for the 15 August 1552 interview with the king that led to

Bale's appointment to the see of Ossory; his patron, John Ponet, was among the signatories of the letter of appointment from the privy council on the following day.

The *Vocacyon* records Bale's experience from the time of his appointment to the bishopric of Ossory until the payment of the ransom that won his freedom little more than a year later at the outset of his second Continental exile. It documents continual conflict between an uncompromising missionary bishop and the Irish clergy, upon whom he vented hostility because of their breaking of religious vows, and the people whom he attempted to convert from "papistry." It records the poisoning of Archbishop Goodacre; Bale's staging of his own polemical plays at the market cross in Kilkenny "to the small contentacion of the prestes and other papistes there" (ll. 977–78); the killing of English Protestants; the murder of his servants for obeying his orders to mow hay on the feast day of the Nativity of Our Lady; his ostensible delivery from murderous priests; and his kidnapping by a Flemish pirate who took Bale "a roavinge" (l. 1536), threatened to turn him over to Queen Mary's privy council, and held him under conditions that enabled him to become "so full of lyce / as I coulde swarme" (l. 1680). The work has a retrospective quality because it is addressed as a consolatory text to the believers who make up the "sorowfull churche of Englande / that in the middes of thy afflictions thu shuldest not despayre" (ll. 1775–77). Running through the entire text is the comforting theme that the suffering of English Protestants under Queen Mary is only the latest incident in a cyclical pattern of suffering followed by providential deliverance, which underlies the history of the "true" church from its earliest origins. Bale assures his audience that its setbacks constitute a test of faith that will inevitably be followed by new cause for rejoicing. Even though Bale has not suffered to the point of martyrdom, like other Protestant saints, he offers his experience as an exemplary testimonial of how the persecuted faithful may "beholde how gracyously our most mercyfull God wyth hys power wayteth upon them / and fynally delyvereth them in most depe daungers" (ll. 14–17).

During the five years of his second exile, Bale took refuge in different locations on the Continent, where he continued to write a variety of tracts. He joined his associate John Foxe in Basel, where their writings were published by Joannes Oporinus; Foxe found employment as a proofreader at the press. At this location Bale completed the expansion of his *Summarium* into the two folio volumes of *Catalogus* (Basel, 1557–59). His *Acta Romanorum Pontificum* (Basel, 1558) complements that massive bibliographical text by providing an extended antipapal history that he assimilates into the historical framework of the *Catalogus*. Returning to his homeland for the last time after the accession of Queen Elizabeth, Bale received a prebend at Canterbury Cathedral from Archbishop Matthew Parker, with whom he collaborated as an antiquarian. At this time, the queen ordered Warham and Robert St. Leger to return books and writings to Bale, "a man that hath byn studious in the serche for the history and antiquities of this our realme." These individuals were respectively the son and brother of Sir Anthony St. Leger, who was Lord Deputy for Ireland when Bale's library presumably came into his hands. The *Vocacyon* corroborates the queen's claim that Bale abandoned his historical research "in the tyme of our late sister Quene Mary, when he was occasioned to departe out of Ireland." The royal order states that the return of these possessions is in the national interest "for the illustration and setting forth of the storye of this our realme by him, the said Bale."[10] He complained bitterly to Archbishop Parker that the St. Legers failed to return his property. Bale had not undertaken the work envisioned in the queen's order when he died in 1563 at the age of sixty-eight. Parker evidently purchased part of the collection after his death, because he lent some of Bale's manuscripts to Matthias Flacius Illyricus on the condition that they be returned within one year.[11] In the *Vocacyon* Bale refers to the interest that Flacius and other Continental reformers had taken in the manuscripts Bale had collected and catalogued (ll. 1571–75).

Genre, Sources, and Analogues

Bale's *Vocacyon* represents a precursor of the spiritual autobiographies that became fashionable within Puritan circles during the seventeenth century. It offers an unusually detailed account of a turbulent year as an example of God's providential deliverance of a Protestant "saint." Literary antecedents include the visions of Juliana of Norwich (c. 1343-c. 1413) and *The Book of Margery Kempe* (c. 1436), the earliest autobiographical narrative extant in the English language. Unlike these illiterate medieval mystics, who had to rely upon amanuenses, Bale wrote his *Vocacyon* on his own, and presumably arranged for its publication. The hundreds of entries in the *Summarium* and *Catalogus* offer a precedent for this work because they contain a brief biography and character for each author, in addition to a bibliography. Treating individual authors as exemplary types within the overarching movement of providential history, Bale gives himself a place of honor in the *Summarium* by positioning his own rudimentary autobiography at the end of that collection. The *Vocacyon* lacks the degree of self-reflection found in *The Book of Margery Kempe*, and the intense analysis of individual consciousness found in later autobiographies, but it shares the tendency of late sixteenth- and seventeenth-century Puritan diaries and confessional works to examine the experience of the self for marks of divine intervention and the operation of grace.[12] The *Vocacyon* has the mixed character found in Bunyan's *Grace Abounding* (1666) and *Reliquiae Baxterianae: or Mr. Richard Baxter's Narrative of the Most Memorable Passages of his Life and Times* (1696) because it assimilates overlapping elements from a variety of genres including chronicle, religious tract, exemplum, and saint's life.

The *Vocacyon* has been termed "an autobiographical saint's life" because Bale dramatizes his experience along the lines of his editions of the martyrologies of Sir John Oldcastle and Anne Askew. Like those texts, it vilifies persecutors and offers examples for the faithful to follow in resisting persecution.[13] Bale calls attention to ways in which his own suffering and the persecution of "true" believers have been followed by divine deliverance and rejoicing. His extensive knowledge of and reliance upon the English chronicles that he collected and studied so assiduously (see note 11) conditioned his effort to place his own experience and that of his beleaguered co-religionists within the context of providential history. At roughly the time that Bale was composing the *Vocacyon*, John Foxe had already begun work on the massive collection of martyrologies that resulted in the 1563 publication of the "Book of Martyrs." His account of the flight into exile of Catherine Brandon, dowager Duchess of Suffolk, offers certain parallels to Bale's experience as an exile.

The Bible provides the outstanding literary model for Bale's writings. He rarely refers to the classics. Bale shares the undiluted scripturalism of other Edwardian "gospellers" and many later Protestants, who integrate profuse biblical quotation, allusion, and paraphrase into their literary works. (Scripturalism is also an aspect of late medieval writing.) While he sometimes quotes directly from the Tyndale translation (or the Great Bible, through which it was mediated), very often he paraphrases roughly or gives a simple reference to a passage. Upon occasion he quotes from the Vulgate Bible, possibly from memory because the references are rarely, if ever, exact. (Bale's plays also contain quotations from the Vulgate.) He would have known the Latin scriptures intimately during his membership in the Carmelite order.

The Bible furnishes many models for the typological pattern of the suffering of the persecuted faithful and their providential deliverance, into which Bale casts his experience and that of his fellow reformers. The Revelation prophecies that he interpreted as foreshadowings of the history of the Christian church in the *Image of Both Churches* provide the overarching pattern for the conflict between "The English Christian" and "The Irishe Papist" that is crystallized in the woodcut appearing on the title page. Although "these troublouse dayes" during the reign of Queen Mary represent a major setback for "true" religion (l. 64), Bale looks back to the reigns of Henry VIII and Edward VI for consolation. Thus he idealizes Henry as a new David for expelling the pope as "the great Golias [i.e., Goliath] of Rome," just as he sees the late king Edward as a second Solomon who labored to erect a Temple in the New Jerusalem of Reformation England. Although the return to "popysh religyon" under Mary recalls backsliding under Jeroboam, when Israel returned to idolatry, Old Testament precedents hold out the prospect of succession by a reforming monarch like Asa or Josiah. Bale may have anticipated the possibility that Princess Elizabeth would undo the Marian reaction if it were possible for her to ascend to the throne (ll. 577–96).

Bale's enduring typological theme is the identification of his own experience and that of other English reformers with New Testament antitypes, notably the voyages of St. Paul and the missions among the Gentiles that brought the apostle to his death in Rome. Bale consistently views himself as a latter-day St. Paul, although he acknowledges that he "be farre unlyke" him (ll. 66–68). The persecutions experienced by the apostle provide a model for the fundamental pattern of suffering and deliverance that Bale perceives in his own fortunes as a bishop in Ireland, just as Paul's divine calling to undertake a mission among the Gentiles furnishes a prototype for Bale's appointment "in this age / to preache the same Gospel to the Irishe heathens" (ll. 92–93). Likewise Paul's escape from Damascus by means of his disciples' stratagem of lowering him from the city walls in a basket offers a model for Bale's flight from Dublin by night in disguise as a sailor. He identifies the large armed escort that enabled him to escape from Holmes Court with the company of soldiers that the Roman tribune provided to accompany Paul from Jerusalem to Caesarea (ll. 146–61). Bale concludes that his flight to Germany recapitulates Paul's final voyage to Rome because of the many parallels in the experiences of the two Christian ministers expelled from their spiritual homelands to wander among enemies and experience the danger of imminent martyrdom: "Thus had I in my troublous journaye from Irelande into Germanye all those chaunces in a maner that S. Paul had in his journaie of no lesse trouble / from Jerusalem to

Rome / saving that we lost not our shippe by the waye" (ll. 213–17).

The *Vocacyon* has an affinity with the tradition of anticlerical complaint and satire that flourished during the later Middle Ages and Reformation. The entries in the *Summarium* and *Catalogus* for the writings of Chaucer (whom Bale and his colleagues viewed as a Wyclifite reformer), William (or Robert) Langland, Walter Map, Nigel Wirecker (see note on l. 537), Simon Fish, Luke Shepherd, and Robert Crowley demonstrate the author's familiarity with the themes and conventions of native English satire. The vignettes of licentious and avaricious clerics like the priest known as "Syr Philypp," who boasted of his illegitimate parentage by the late prior of the house of the White Friars in Knocktopher (ll. 687–700), and the Cornish priest known as "Sir James," who is alleged to have fathered bastards in order "to encreace the churches profyght in crisyms and offeringes" (ll. 1475–79), have a satirical edge like that found in Chaucer's portrayal of worldly clerics like the Monk and Friar. Bale shares the tendency of his contemporary, Luke Shepherd, to heap up scatological and sexual innuendo in vigorously colloquial catalogues that employ what later readers regarded as obscenity in attacking clerical abuses. A work like Shepherd's *Doctour Doubble Ale* (c. 1548) fictionalizes behavior that corresponds to Bale's attacks on the drunkenness of the clergy of Kilkenny (ll. 877–81) and on Archbishop Browne for boasting "upon his ale benche with the cuppe in his hande" (ll. 1299–1300).[14] These writings recall the satirical attacks on tavern-haunting clergy that inform goliardic poetry. Clerical vices of this kind are cited in Bale's edition of *Apocalypsis Goliae*, a satire attributed to Walter Map, under the title of *Rhithmi vetustissimi de corrupto ecclesiae statu* (Antwerp, 1546).[15]

The central part of the *Vocacyon* (ll. 597–1731) — just over half the work — is written in a style rare for its directness, and explicit in many minute details. Apart from occasional emphatic polemical asides, it is essentially a realistic personal narrative of Bale's election, his residence in Ireland, and his escape. Several specific dates are given, notably that of his visit to Southampton commencing on 15 August 1552, which is the beginning of the narrative, and a group of references from 25 July 1553, when the news of King Edward's death reached Ireland, to 8 September of the same year, when Bale's servants were murdered. For these critical periods Bale may have been working from a diary. The subsequent sea voyage is given in some chronological detail. This part is especially readable for the way in which Bale gives brief character sketches, and for the lively accounts of conversations reported with tart immediacy. It may well be that the style of this part—rare for its period—gives some useful evidence of the sensitive appreciation of language that informs the dialogue of his plays.

Religion

Bale's appointment as an Irish bishop, like that of Hugh Goodacre as Archbishop of Armagh, accorded with the increasingly radical religious climate that followed the deposition of Protector Somerset by the Earl of Warwick. Bale was sent to Ossory as part of a concerted English plan to convert the Irish to Protestantism.[16] His major religious concerns are the purgation of clerical abuses and the proper education of the laity in the creed and ritual of the church. In line with the Protestant doctrine of the "priesthood of all believers," he joins other reformers in denying the extreme sacerdotalism that came to dominate the Roman church by the late Middle Ages. On the ground that the Reformation constitutes an effort to return to practices followed by the "primative churche" immediately after the apostolic age (1. 358), he insists that the "papists" perverted true faith by introducing superstitious beliefs lacking a scriptural foundation. Accordingly, Roman monasticism was a chief agent in England's subversion by Antichrist because it substituted "fantastical doctrines / vaine tradicions / and supersticiouse ordinaunces" for the preaching of "Gods heavenly wurde" (ll. 530–31).

Chief among alleged "papist" abuses are the doctrine of transubstantiation and the Roman rite for the mass, which introduce "worshippinge of breade and of wyne" in place of a communion service designed to commemorate Christ's sacrifice and to draw communicants into "one misticall bodie in Christe" (ll. 377–84). His repeated charge that "papist" clergy err "for their bellies sake" (ll. 82–83, 533, 669, 729) conflates the attack against the mass with charges against priestly hedonism. Fundamental to both these alleged errors is the abandonment of pastoral "feeding" of the congregation with scriptural truth in favor of coarsely material feeding and digestion (see ll. 385–92). Corollary to the epicureanism of the clergy is the violation of vows of celibacy that resulted in the substitution of "monstruouse buggery for a professed virginite" (ll. 545–46). As a married bishop, like his colleagues at the sees of Kildare and Leighlin, Bale enthusiastically endorses the Protestant attack on the medieval ideal of celibacy. He describes his unsuccessful campaign to persuade the priests of his diocese to marry (ll. 811–36), on the grounds that celibacy not only lacks scriptural authority, but corrupts the clergy because it encourages priests to break the Seventh Commandment by committing fornication, adultery, and sodomy.

The title of Bale's book reflects the urgency of his concern to define his clerical vocation, and by extension that of any "true" minister, as a direct "calling" by God to preach biblical truth and to administer what Protestants regard as the two sacraments of communion and baptism. Divine election is as essential to a clerical career as it is to the salvation of the faithful. Christ is the chief model for the ministry, but Jeremiah, John the Baptist, and St. Paul also furnish biblical precedents for the "heavenly offyce of preachynge" (ll. 51–53). By viewing his own appointment as Bishop of Ossory in evangelical terms as a charge "purely to preache the Gospell of God / to his christened flocke" (ll. 10–11), Bale attacks the separation of clergy from laity that led to the denial of pastoral care and the profligacy of the princely popes and bishops of the late Middle Ages. By frequently delivering sermons during his Irish tenure, he denied the widespread belief that bishops were entitled to live luxurious lives remote from parishioners.

Bale approves of the choice of bishops and control of the ecclesiastical hierarchy by Henry VIII and Edward VI. Their rejection of the Bishop of Rome as the primate of the church through direct inheritance from St. Peter has restored, in his view, the direct apostolic succession of the Church of England from Christ and the early church. According to Bale's legendary historical sources, Christianity was transmitted directly to Britain from the original gospel source by Joseph of Arimathea, a secret disciple of Christ, whose arrival predated the mission from Rome of St. Augustine of Canterbury: "From the schole of Christe hymselfe / have we receyved the documentes of oure fayth. From Jerusalem / & not from Rome / whom both Peter & also Christe hath called Babylon / for that she so aptely therunto agreeth in ministryng confusion to the world" (ll. 462–66). Joseph established a line of true believers, including Wyclif and Tyndale, who nurtured the "Brittish churche in the doctrine of faithe / without mennes [i.e., nonscriptural] tradicions" (ll. 485–86).

Bale perceives Ireland as a hotbed of religious abuses on the part of both the clergy and the "poore people [who] are not taught / but mocked of their mynysters" (ll. 1502–3). Upon his arrival in Waterford, for example, he blames the presence of "heathnysh" behavior (l. 679) on the absence of a good bishop and the excesses of "Epicurysh prestes" (l. 668). He displays special hostility to the substitution of ritual and song ("chauntynge / pypynge / and syngynge") for the "true" ministerial vocation of preaching and instructing "the people in the doctryne and wayes of God" (ll. 807–10). Ceremonialism errs in the same way as the traditional mass and Vulgate Bible by failing to contribute to the spiritual education of the average parishioner. The beliefs that Bale attempts to disseminate, against the stiff opposition of the local clergy in Ossory, reflect the practicalities of active evangelism and pulpit preaching rather than learned theology. Thus he sums up the core of religion in admonitions that the people repent of their sins, worship God alone, and maintain faith in Christ as the sole redeemer of humanity. Christ's salvation of souls without any need of clerical or saintly intercession denies the validity of purgatory, celebration of masses for the dead, and devotion to the cult of saints (ll. 788–810). Although the first *Book of Common Prayer* (1549) provided the only legal order of worship for use in Ireland, Bale imposed the use of the second prayer book of 1552 in his diocese; it rendered the traditional mass illegal. His arguments led to the use of the second prayer book at his consecration as bishop, even though he charges that Archbishop Browne went "about that observacion / very unsaverly and as one not muche exercised in that kinde of doynge" (ll. 751–52).

Reception

No record survives of how English Protestants responded to the *Vocacyon*, but two apologists for Queen Mary vilified the text. Miles Hogarde includes the work in a general attack against the writings of Bale and his fellow reformers in *The Displaying of the Protestantes* (1556), a polemic in which this "servant to the Quenes majestie" defends the burning of Protestants as heretics. In a reversal of scriptural typology that Bale had applied in praise of Henry VIII and Edward VI, Hogarde defends the return to religious orthodoxy in the New Israel of Counter Reformation England. James Cancellar condemns Bale as a renegade friar and attacks other Protestant dissidents in *The Pathe of Obedience, righte necessarye for all the king and quenes majesties loving subjectes* (1556?), a work that he wrote as a member of the Marian establishment. As chaplain to Queen Mary, he dedicates the text to his patroness. Like Hogarde, he compares the reformers' disobedience to the rebelliousness of the Israelites against Moses (sig. B8ᵛ). Cancellar includes many specific folio references to the *Vocacyon* in his heated rebuttal of Bale's comparison of his own experience and that of some members of his faction to the actions of St. Paul and other New Testament antitypes (see Appendix). The orthodox arguments that both Hogarde and Cancellar lodge against disobedience and rebellion accord with views that Protestant apologists had articulated under Henry VIII and Edward VI in works like Sir John Cheke's *The Hurt of Sedicion* (1549). Cancellar's conservative position in favor of the absolute obedience of subject to ruler shows no awareness of the revolutionary step taken by the contemporary Protestant exile, John Ponet, in advocating the justness of tyrannicide as a response to persecution.[17] It should be noted that Bale, as an advocate of royal supremacy, never followed his former patron in accepting this radical shift in political theory.

A Note on the Text

The Vocacyon (STC 1307), according to the colophon, was printed in 1553, very shortly after the adventures described in it were over. The place of printing is allegedly Rome, though this is an impudent joke. The types used were 82 Textura ("a thin Low Countries type") and 80 Roman, as illustrated by F. S. Isaac, *English and Scottish Printing Types, 1535–1552, 1552–58* (Oxford, 1932), Fig. 117. These types appeared in the "Michael Wood" pamphlet *De vera obedientia* (STC 11587) which was also allegedly produced at Rome in November 1553. The printer's device on G8^v belongs to Hugh Singleton, and it seems likely that he actually printed it at Wesel, the place of Bale's first exile in 1540–48. However, if Miss Christina Garrett is right about Singleton's imprisonment in the Tower of London with John Day, another known Protestant printer, from about October 1553, the printing must have taken place later than the colophon claims. This would not be out of keeping with Bale's desire to print his account with apparently miraculous haste after his deliverance. The woodcut on the title page was in the possession of Joos Lambrecht, who was at work in Wesel from the second half of 1553 until 1556, and it may demonstrate a joint enterprise with Singleton. The Douce copy (D) contains a note that this cut also appeared in a Flemish poem "Een zuverlic boucxkin" printed at Ghent in 1543. There is a second woodcut on A8^v which shows Veritas holding a torch and a book inscribed "verbum dei."

The edition has an index, G1ᵛ–G7ᵛ, a page of corrections, G8, and some quotations translated from Psalms 31 and 59 on G8ᵛ. These pages have no folio numbers.

Large capitals (black letter, approximately 10–12mm) are used for the first letter of the text of the Preface (fol. 2), for part of the heading and first letter of the main text (fol. 9), for the first letter of the Conclusion (fol. 43), and for the first letter of each alphabetical section of the Table (G1ᵛ–G7ᵛ). Bold type appears in a number of places, mostly for lists of personal names, and for some Latin quotations. One special occurrence is for biblical names having a special contemporary relevance that Bale wished to point up (fol. 44^{r-v}).

Davies gives the collation: 8° A–G^8 Ff. 49 + [7], black letter.

There was no other sixteenth-century edition, though a riposte by James Cancellar appeared in *The Pathe of Obedience* (see Appendix), and there is a further reply by Bale in Lambeth Palace MS 2001 (autograph). *The Vocacyon* was reprinted in *The Harleian Miscellany* in 1744 and again in 1808. Extracts appeared in *Writings of John Fox, Bale and Coverdale* (London, 1831: British Library cat. 865. c. 5).

The following copies are known:

C   Cambridge University Library, Hib.8.55.1. "Alice Browne's Book 1708," (fol. 1ᵛ). "From Mr. Browne's books at Stonesfield."

B   The Queen's University, Belfast. Acquired from Dr. Samuel Simms in 1960. Imperfect, wants fols. 41 and 43–48.

D   Bodleian, Douce B300. Bale's portrait from his *Catalogus* (1557) has been inserted as a frontispiece, but there is no justification for the old STC division into two editions. This copy is on STC microfilm, Reel 171 (See textual note to l. 770).

Hn   Huntington Library, San Marino, California. This copy is on STC microfilm, Reel 485.

L   British Library, c.37.b.5. Margins cropped. "This is John Cruse his Booke dwelling in Grub Strete, 1586."

La   Lambeth Palace Library, 1550.06.8. Bound with seven other Protestant items, the first being *An Epistle to the right honorable Duke of Somerset* (1550): the binding is stamped with the arms of Archbishop Bancroft, who founded the Library in 1610. Lacks title page. Front and back sheets dirtied.

Li   Lincoln Cathedral Library, SS.6.14. Probably collected for the library by Michael Honywood, Dean of Lincoln 1660–71, perhaps in the Low Countries. Title page (fol. 1) torn out, with stub in binding.

M   Bodleian, Mason AA27. Type very clear. Margins cropped.

Ml   Bodleian, Malone 504. Margins cropped. Duplicate sale from British Museum 1787.

T   Trinity College, Cambridge, C.7.53. Came into the library between 1747 and 1875. Margins heavily cropped.

A copy is recorded in A. Maunsell, *First Part of the Catalogue of English Printed Books* (Lothbury, London, 1595).

It is possible to trace some of the relationships among the extant copies, but any consideration of this ought to start from McKerrow's dictum that it is very difficult to conceive of one comprehensively corrected copy of an early printed book since the selection of the sheets or gathers by the binder might not be made following the order of correction. The surviving copies of *The Vocacyon* illustrate this.

Of the corrections listed on G8, the first two were made in all the copies except B. (In Hn the remaining corrections have been interpolated by hand in ink.) Thus the press variants occur at the following places (full details are in the Textual Notes below):

i.	60	I am
ii.	179	at Melita
iii.	194	drowned
iv.	217	waye.
v.	246	wonderfull
vi.	249–50	God / which
vii.	251	me / and
viii.	282	DOMINI
ix.	1405	but

All but the last are on the first sheet (sig. A), and it is clear that there are three states of this sheet:

1. The first is represented by B where all the eight later variants are in the original state.

2. The second is exemplified in D, L, La, M, Ml which have nos. ii and iii, and nos. v, vi, vii corrected (grouped on A6 and A7^v).

3. The third state, as in C, Hn, Li, and T, incorporates all five corrections in the second state, and adds nos. i, iv, and viii.

It is not possible to continue this analysis with the majority of the other sheets because there are no other variants except no. ix. From this latter one can say that sheet E has two states. L and M have *bnt* at 1405, whereas all the other copies have *but*. This precludes the assumption that the whole of B is an earlier copy.

In summary, the relationship between the copies must be based on the following:

B contains the first version of sheet A and the later version of E.

L, M contain the second state of A and the earlier E.

Ml, La, D have the second state of A and the later E.

C, Hn, Li, T have the third state of A and the later E.

The reprints in *The Harleian Miscellany* (Harl.) have *am I* following the uncorrected state (variant i.), but *DOMINI* (variant viii.) has been corrected, presumably because the item had to be re-set in omitting the woodcut. All the corrections required on G8 were made in these reprints, and obvious printer's errors were eliminated, including the press variant *bnt* at 1405. The Index and other supplementary matter are omitted. In general Harl. offers no independent evidence about the original. There are many discrepancies, some to correct or update the original and some occasioned by the difficulty of reconciling or even recording inconsistencies in the original, particularly final *e* and *i/y.* These have been ignored here. The Harleian reprints may well derive from L or Ml (which was in the British Museum until 1787).

References

W. T. Davies, "A Bibliography of John Bale," *Oxford Bibliographical Society Proceedings and Papers* 5 (1940): 203–79.

L. P. Fairfield, "The Mysterious Press of 'Michael Wood' (1553–54)," *The Library,* 5th ser., 27 (1972): 220–32, especially note 10.

Christina H. Garrett, *"The Resurrection of the Masse,* by Hugh Hilarie — or John Bale?" *The Library,* 4th ser., 21 (1941): 143–59.

R. B. McKerrow, *An Introduction to Bibliography* (Oxford, 1927), 209–10.

Editorial Procedure

All the listed copies have been collated for this edition. The intention has been to print the original *literatim,* taking C as the copy text on the ground that it incorporates all the contemporary corrections. Exceptions to this are that modern practice has been followed for *u / v* and *i / j* in accordance with the policy of the Society. Macrons have been expanded silently to the most frequent usage in the text. Other abbreviations have been expanded similarly:

$y^t \rightarrow$ that; $y^e \rightarrow$ the; $w^t \rightarrow$ with; $w^c \rightarrow$ which.

ʃ has been changed to modern s. Numerals have been left in the original forms, inconsistencies as between roman and arabic being preserved. However some stops have been eliminated in parenthetical scripture references.

The abbreviations fo. and fol. (for "folio") have been standardized to fol. throughout.

Emendations, for spelling and other reasons, are in square brackets, with the original in the notes. Turned or transposed letters and the infrequent re-division of spaces have been treated silently in the text, but the original forms are noted. Occasionally it is very difficult to distinguish between u and n. The errata recorded on G8 have been put right *in situ*, enclosed in square brackets. An asterisk (*) has been used to distinguish the notes relevant to these errata.

In the original one passage of about three lines (618–20) was repeated from the foot of fol. 16 to the head of fol. 16^v. The second version has been taken as definitive on the authority of G8. A few cases of excessive wear to type have been noted. An attempt to replace damaged type was made in press on fol. 2^v (40, 41). Marginal subheadings have been retained, and are placed at a point corresponding to the first word in the relevant line of the original.

Paragraphing and Punctuation

In general few alterations have been made to these in the present text. The original has its own conventions which ought to be respected since differences from modern practices may very well have rhetorical significance.

Paragraphing. The paragraphing of the original texts is rather unsystematic. The amount of indent for the first words varies from the width of about two letters to the width of about four. In a number of cases new paragraphs have been printed with the first word not indented. Both these inconsistencies have been given standard indents, except at 83, 474, 1000, 1023, 1071, 1120, and 1121 where the sense precludes a paragraph break and the text is run on in this edition.

Punctuation. Certain sixteenth-century features are regular in the original, and have been allowed to stand. These include the following words commonly beginning sentences which, in modern practice, might be used as conjunctions or relative pronouns:

Which:	e.g., 63, 489, 537
For:	e.g., 68, 74, 514
Where as:	e.g., 1363
Like:	e.g., 2029
And:	e.g., 84
So that	e.g., 2010

Direct speech following a verb of speaking or reporting usually begins with a capital (109). Phrases like "sayth the baylyfe" (1433) are normally in brackets. The practice for questions in reported speech and in reported quotations is for a mark of interrogation to follow the spoken words: I axed him / if that were in marriage? (691 and *passim*).

Some passages containing lists of parallels, which would be arranged as a long sentence in modern style, are separated into individual units by full stops (786, 788, 1012–28). "Item" is used similarly at 997.

The original does not use the exclamation mark, contrary to modern practice: "O right Antichristes [!]" (1212–13). Some sentences which introduce a topic in argument are imperfect: To fatche this thinge from the first foundacion / for that lande / lyke as for other landes. (398–99, cf. 300). The virgule (/) is used in the original to carry out the functions of the comma and the colon in modern English. It is retained in this edition since it has both syntactical and rhetorical significance. The use of upper and lower case *s* with the names of saints is inconsistent in the copy. Although this does not seem to have any polemical significance, these letters are retained here in their original form.

The following items have been changed in the interest of intelligibility or consistency with the conventions of the text:

54 yea
88 sayde.
90 .what
165 .So
306 Noe
314 Arabia.
381 holiest.
417 .Helthe
474 chaptre
508 sharply,
513 .Than
535 .As
602–3 .I
643 frendes.
735 sayde.
800 ,Much
863 nomore.
930 .Myndinge

1000 prestes,
1019 [2]him.
1023 creature.
1037 deservinges.
1039 scriptures.
1048 them.
1071 .An ([1]an)
1121 ? They
1227 them.
1256 I
1278 wolde
1386 Captayne.
1452 displeasure.
1462 saienge.
1490 me.
1849 .well
1852 .yea
1885 sayth.
1931 sumtyme.

Notes to Introduction

1. *Catalogus* 1:title page, 702.
2. John Sherman, "Aborigines Jesuani," Jesus College, Cambridge MS (c. 1660).
3. *Catalogus* 1:702. See James K. McConica, *English Humanists and Reformation Politics under Henry VIII and Edward VI* (Oxford: Clarendon Press, 1965), 219.
4. "The answer of John Bale pryst unto serten artycles unjustlye gadred upon hys prechyng," Public Record Office, SP 1/111, fols. 183–87.
5. *Catalogus* 1:702.
6. David Bevington, *Tudor Drama and Politics: A Critical Approach to Topical Meaning* (Cambridge, Mass.: Harvard Univ. Press, 1968), 97–98.
7. On the Protestant assault against the Catholic church as "a demonic parody of the true church," see Stephen Greenblatt, *Renaissance Self-Fashioning: From More to Shakespeare* (Chicago: Univ. of Chicago Press, 1980), 81.
8. See Katharine R. Firth, *The Apocalyptic Tradition in Reformation Britain, 1530–1645* (Oxford: Oxford Univ. Press, 1979), 42.
9. *A Brefe Chronycle concernynge the Examinacyon of Syr Johan Oldecastell* (Antwerp, 1544); *The First Examinacyon of Anne Askewe* (Marburg, i.e., Wesel, 1546); and *The Lattre Examinacyon of Anne Askewe* (Marburg, i.e., Wesel, 1547). See Peter Happé, "The Protestant Adaptation of the Saint Play," in Clifford Davidson, ed., *The Saint Play in Medieval Europe* (Kalamazoo, 1986), 205–40.
10. *Calendar of State Papers Relating to Ireland (1509–1603)*, 10 vols. (1860–1912), 1 (1509–73):158.

11. Honor McCusker, "Books and Manuscripts Formerly in the Possession of John Bale," *Library*, 4th ser., 16 (1935), 146–48. Some of Bale's books with his autograph notes are in the Parker Library at Corpus Christi College, Cambridge.

12. See Owen C. Watkins, *The Puritan Experience* (London: Routledge and Kegan Paul, 1972), 18–28, 101–20, passim.

13. Leslie P. Fairfield, "*The vocacyon of Johan Bale* and Early English Autobiography," *Renaissance Quarterly* 24 (1971): 327–28, 332–33. He cites Bale's attack on *The Golden Legend* in *A Mysterye of Inyquyte* (Antwerp, 1545): "Nothynge els are youre histories of the Saintes but fables / lyes / and fantasyes taken out of Legenda aurea made by fryre James de Voragine" (sig. I4^v).

14. On Bale's knowledge of the writings of Shepherd and other satirists, see *Summarium*, R1^r, Z4^r, 3F4^v; and *Catalogus* 1:245–46, 253, 474–75, 525–27, 728–29; 2:102, 109.

15. On the continuity of anticlerical satire written in the late Middle Ages and Reformation, see John Peter, *Complaint and Satire in Early English Literature* (Oxford: Clarendon Press, 1956), 80–83; and *ERL*, 252–70, 387–406, and passim. See also *Laws* 1766–68; *KJ* 2086–91.

16. R. Dudley Edwards, *Ireland in the Age of the Tudors: The Destruction of Hiberno-Norman Civilization* (London: Croom Helm, 1977), 64, 71.

17. *A Shorte Treatise of Politike Power* (Strasbourg, 1556), chap. 6.

The vocacyon
of Johan Bale

The vocacyon
of Johā Bale to the
bishopzick of Ossozie in Jre
lāde his persecuciōs in ÿ same/₹
finall delpueraunce.

The English Christiā / The Jrishe Papist.

❧ God hath deliuered me from the snare of the
hunter/₹ frō ÿ noysome pestilēce. Psal.xcj.
❧ Jf J must nedes reioyce/J wil reioyce
of myne infirmytees. ij. Coz.xj.

The vocacyon

of Johã Bale to the

bishoprick of Ossorie in Ire

lãde his persecuciõs in the same / &
finall delyberaunce.

(Device)

The English Christiã / The Irishe Papist.

¶God hath delivered me from the snare of the
hunter / & frõ the noysome pestilēce. Psal. xci.
¶If I must nedes reioyce / I wil reioyce
of myne infirmytees. ii. Cor. xi.

The Preface.
Johan Bale to the folowers of Christes Gospell.

FOr thre consyderacyons chefely (dere bretherne) have I
put fourth thys treatyse of my vocacyon to the churche 5
of Ossorye in Irelande / of my harde chaunces therin / and Ossorie
of my fynall deliveraunce by the great goodnesse of God. The
first of them is / for that men shulde wele knowe / that the
office of a Christen byshop / is not to loyter in blasphemouse 9
papistrie / but purely to preache the Gospell of God / to his
christened flocke. The seconde is / that they shulde also The
understande / that contynuall persecucyons / and no bodyly flocke
welthe / doeth folowe the same most godly office / in them
which truly executeth it. The thirde is / that they myght beholde how gracyously our most mercyfull God wyth hys 15
power wayteth upon them / and fynally delyvereth them Delive-
in most depe daungers. raunce.
These .3. thynges notable / concerninge the electe membres
of Gods congregacyon in thys life / comprehendeth muche
matter in the scriptures of both testamentes / with abun- 20
daunce of examples from Abel the first to Johan the evan-
gelyst / which was the last lyver in the same. fol. 2^V Aii^V
The examples also therof are both lyvely and innumerable Examples
/ in the first propagacion and longe contynuaunce of the

25 christen churche from hys tyme to thys our tyme / as the
chronycles & hystoryes most abundauntly specifieth.

Jesus.   First / as concernynge the examples of holye scripture. Jesus
Adam. the eternall sonne of the everlastynge father / in the God-
hede preached to Adam in paradyse terrestre / and consty-
30 tute hym so wele an instructour as a father over hys posteryte.
He proved him also after he had sinned / by dyverse afflyc-
tyons / and fynally promysed both to hym and to hys / deliveraunce in the sede of the woman / which at the lattre in hys
Christe owne persone he lovingly perfourmed. Christe the seyde sonne
35 of God contynually still taught / by the mouthes of the fathers
and prophetes / tyll suche tyme as he hymselfe came in the
fleshe. Than was he above all others / of hys heavenly father
appoynted / a universall doctor over all the worlde / and com-
A doctour maunded to be hearde / (Math. iii). He folowed hys vocacyon
40 in most ample wyse / very cruelly was he of the clergie than
persecuted / and gloriously delyvered in hys resurrectyon from
deathe. The members of hys true churche / the prophetes and
fol. 3 Aiii Apostles / were in case like as he their head was / first called
Fathers / than afflicted / and gracyously alwayes in the ende dely-
45 vered. He that shall marke the laboriouse procedinges of Abraham / Joseph / & Moyses / of David / Helyas / and Daniel
/ with the other olde fathers and prophetes / shall fynde it
no lesse. He lyke wyse that shall dyscretely searche the
doynges of Peter / James and Johan / with the other of the
50 Apostles and dysciples / shall wele perceyve the same.

   Hieremye for the olde lawe / Paule for the newe lawe / and
Called. Johan Baptyst betwixt them both / were called from their
mothers wombe to that heavenly offyce of preachynge (Hier.
i, Luce. i, Gala. i). Yea / they suffered extreme persecucyons
55 undre tyrauntes / and fynally were delivered / in this lyfe
from parelouse daungers/ and in deathe / from synne / helle
/ and dampnacyon. To rehearce the examples of the prima-
Ages. tyve churche / and of the ages folowynge / concernynge these
matters / it wolde requyre muche tyme / they are so manye
60 / and therfor at thys present I omit them. Thus I am not alone
in these 3. matters of vocacion / persecucion / & deliver-
The au- aunce / but have on my syde an infinyte nombre of exam-
thor. ples. Which maketh me the more a great dele to rejoyce / like

as I wishe them to do / which have in these troublouse dayes   fol. 3ᵛ Aiiiᵛ
the lyke. Neyther am I ashamed to tell my bretherne / what   65
God hath most graciously done for me / nomor than s. Paule
was for hymselfe in hys owne Epistles / and Luke in the Actes   s. Peter
for saint Peter / though I be farre unlyke them. For I fare lyke
the byrde which is delivered from the snare of the catcher.
He flyeth to a bough / and rejoyceth in his delyveraunce /   70
and even so do I. In the which rejoyce / I make not only my
selfe merye / but also all my lovinge frindes. And as for my
cruel enemyes the papistes / if I make them sorye in the re-   papistes
hearsal of my delyveraunce / I am not yll apayde therof. For
it is better (they saye in Northfolke) that yonge lyddernes wepe   75
/ than olde men. I call them yonge and not olde / for God
is oldar than Sathan / if age maye be attributed to his eter-   Daniel
nyte / as Daniel sayeth it maye / and Christe oldar than the
devyls vycar at Rome / their ungracyouse father.

As we are in most thinges contrarie to these papistes / so   papistes
have we rejoyces contrary to theirs. They rejoyce in helthe   81
/ prosperite / riches and worldly pleasures for their bellies
sake. We in our infirmytees / afflictions / losses / and sorowfull crostes / for Christes veritees sake. And thus maye we
wele do / and boast of it also without offence / for so ded   fol. 4 Aiv
the forenamed S. Paule (2 Cor. 11) and earnestly willed us   s. Paule
to be his folowers (Phil. 3). First he boasted of his vocacion
/ and sayde, God sorted me out and appointed me from my
mothers wombe / and also he called me by his grace / to
preache his lively gospell amonge the heathen / (Gal. 1). What   90
if I shoulde in like case boaste / that he by his grace had also
called me in this age / to preache the same Gospel to the   Irishe.
Irishe heathens / which never hearde of it afore / to
knowledge? I shulde not do other wise than the truthe is. For
I was put to it against my wille / by a most christen kynge   95
/ and of his owne mere mocion only / without sute of fryndes
/ mede / labour / expensis / or any other sinistre meane els.
By his Regall power and authorite / which both were of God   Edward
/ (Ro. 13) was I both allowed and confirmed / and not all un-
joyfully received of the people / which causeth me in con-   100
science to judge my vocacion just. Yet was not my rejoyce so
muche in the dignite therof / as in doinge for the time / the   Office

office therunto belonginge. But now is it most of all in the
leavinge of that bishopricke / the Gospell beinge so unthanke-
105 fully of the prestes received / I so terribly of them persecuted / and my servauntes so cruelly slayne.

fol. 4ᵛ Aivᵛ   Moreover saint Paule boasted muche of his persecucions
S. / and described them at large / concludinge thus in the ende
Paule / Very gladly (saith he) will I rejoyce of my weakenesse / that
110 the strength of Christe maye dwell in me. Therfor have I dilec-
tacion in infirmitees / in rebukes / in nedes / in persecu-
The cion / and anguyshes / for Christes sake (2 Cor. 12). If I have
Author lyke wyse / felte a great meanie of the same afflictions / as
I have done in dede / maye not I also with him rejoyce in
115 them? Maye I not be glad / that I am in sorowes for the Gospell
/ lyke fashioned to him / & not pranked up in pompe &
pleasures / lyke the wanton babes of this worlde? As at this
Weston daye is lecherouse Weston / which is more practised in the
arte of breche burninge / than all the whores of the stues /
120 to the great infamye of his virginall ordre. The truthe of it
is / that sens I toke that wayghtie office in hande / I have
bene sycke to the very deathe / I have bene greved with the
untowardnesse of ministers.

Trou-   I have bene in journayes and labours / in injuryes and losses
bles / in peines and in penuries.

I have bene in strifes and contencions / in rebukynges and
slaunderynges / and in great daunger of poyseninges and kil-
linges.

fol. 5 [Av]   I have bene in parell of the heathen / in parell of wicked
130 prestes / in parell of false justyces / in parell of trayterouse
Tyraun tenauntes / in parell of cursed tyrauntes / in parell of cruell
tes kearnes and galloglasses.

I have bene in parell of the sea / in parell of shypwrack /
in parell of throwynge over the boorde / in parell of false
135 bretherne / in parell of curiouse searchers / in parell of pirates
/ robbers and murtherers / and a great sort more.

Parels   Sanct Paule also rejoyced / that God had so miraculously
delyvered him from so manye daungerouse jeopardyes / and
spareth not so to report them (2 Cor. 11 et 12). Whie shulde
140 I than shrinke or be ashamed to do the lyke / havinge at Gods

hande the lyke miraculouse deliveraunce? Are they not left
to us for example / that we shulde do the lyke whan we fele
the lyke? Whatsoever thinges are written afore tyme (sayth   Written
he) they are written for our learninge / that we through
pacyence and confort of the scriptures might have hope (Rom.   145
xv). He in the cytie of Damascon / beinge layde waite for /
by the liefe tenaunt of Kinge Aretha / was lete downe at a
windowe in a basket / & so escaped his handes (Act. ix).   dubline
I in the cytie of Dubline / beinge assaulted of papistes / was
convayed awaye in the nyght in mariners apparell / & so   150
escaped that daunger by Gods helpe. Whan Paules death was   fol. 5ᵛ [Avᵛ]
sought by certayn Jewes at Jerusalem / the upper captaine
there / commaunded ii under captaines / in the nyght to   Cesarea
conveye him to Cesarea with 200 souldyers, 70 horsmen /
and 200 spearemen / and so to delyver him (Actes. 23). In   155
lycke case / whan the prestes whith Barnabe Bolgar and other
had sought my death at Holmes Court / and had slayne .v.
of my howsholde servauntes by their hyred kearnes / the good   Kilken-
suffren of Kylkennie with an hundred horsemen / and 300   nye
fotemen brought me thyder in the night and so delivered me   160
that tyme.

As Paule against his wylle / was put into a shippe of
Adramitium / coupled with other prisoners of Jewrie / con-   Italie
vaied fourth into Italie / and there safely delivered (Act. 27
and 28), so was I & my companyon Thomas against our   165
willes taken into a shippe of Zelande / coupled with frenche
prisoners / convayed furth into Flanders / and so at the lattre
/ safely there delivered. As their shippe was caught betwixt
Candia and Melita / and coulde not resyste the wyndes / so   The winde
was ours betwixt Mylforde Haven / and Waterforde. As they   170
had an excedynge tempeste upon the sea / so had we lykewyse. As they were withoute hope of savegarde / so were we
also.   173

As they feared Syrtes or daungerouse sandy places and   fol. 6 [Avi]
rockes / so ded we. As they were almost famyshed and   Confort
drowned / so were we. As God conforted them / so ded he
us. As they were in conclusion cast into an ylande / so were
we into S. Ives in Cornewale. As the people shewed them

kyndnesse at Melita / so ded they us at the seyd S. Ives. As
180 Paule gave thankes and brake breade amonge them / so ded
Julius we also. As the captayne Julius courteously intreated hym and
gave hym lyberte to go unto hys fryndes at Sydon / and to
refreshe hym / so ded our captayne Cornelis use us very gen-
tilly with all favour and lyberte / what though he had so cur-
185 rishely and cruelly intreated us afore. As Paule was stonge
Walter of a bytyng vyper and not hurte / so was I of that viperous
Walter being most unjustly accused of treason afore the
justices ther / and yet through Gods deliveraunce / not hurte.
As he appealed to Cesar / so ded I to the trone of God.
Rome   As great dyspycyons were among the Jewes at Rome con-
191 cerning Paule / so were there afterwarde amonge the shyppers in our returne to their shippe concerning us. As the souldyers gave counsell to kylle the prisoners / so were there some
of our men that gave counsell to have drowned us for our
fol. 6ᵛ [Aviᵛ] moneye / and of some to have delyvered us up to the coun-
Publius sayll of Englande / in hope of great rewardes. As Publius gen-
tilly received Paule / and by hym was healed of all hys dyseases
/ so ded myne hoste Lambert receyve me also gentylly / and
by me was delyvered from hys vayne beleve of purgatorye /
200 and of other Popysh peltryes. As the people reported Paule to
be a murtherer / and after changed their myndes / and sayde
A God he was a God / so our wycked maryners reported me to be
a most haynous traytour / and yet afterwarde in my delyveraunce called me the servaunt of God. As he was for the hope
205 of Israel ledde into captivite / and at [the] last delivered /
so was I also for the same captived / and in fyne delyvered
Brether into Germanie. As the bretherne met Paule with rejoyce at
ne Appii forum / so ded they me in diverse partes of Duchelande
/ and lawded God for my so miraculouse deliveraunce. As he
210 sayde that he had committed nothyng against the lawe of his
fathers / so saye I also that I have in this acte committed
nothyng against the Apostels and Prophetes doctryne / I
The thanke my Lord God therof. Thus had I in my troublous jour-
author naye from Irelande into Germanye all those chaunces in a
215 maner that S. Paul had in his journaie of no lesse trouble /
fol. 7 [Avii] from Jerusalem to Rome / saving that we lost not our shippe
by the waye.

If Helias / that wether dryven runnegate / remayne now
in a foren lande in penurie with the Sareptysh wydowe whyls Prestes
Baals chatteringe chaplaynes and sorcerouse sacrifiers do dwell 220
styl at home florissing in prosperouse welth / lecherouse ydel-
nesse / and lordely dignite / marvele not of it / for so hath
he done afore. I speake not thys for myne owne part only /
nether utterly exclude I my selfe / but I uttre it also for my For o-
exyled bretherne / of whom a great nombre is at this tyme thers
in Germanie / Denmarcke / and Geneva. The true churche 226
of God had never sumptuouse hospitalles any longe tyme
together but very simple cottages and caves / if ye marke the
sacred hystoryes and auncyent cronicles. The plesaunt pos- Posses-
session / and gorgious dwelling places / have evermor re- sions
mained to the glorious Epicures / the very enemyes alwayes 231
of Christes gospel. We are not now to lerne how to take these
our present afflictions in good part / for we knowe them afore
hande / and have had them long tyme / as it were in an exer- Exercise
cise. Nether are we all barayne of frindely receptacles / for 235
the heavenly doctrynes sake / though our adversaryes in Englande with violence throwe stones at us / and seke utterly
to destroye us. They are truly muche deceived which thinketh fol. 7ᵛ Aviiᵛ
the Christen churche to be a politicall commen welthe / as churche
of Rome and Constantinople / mayntayned by humayne poly- 240
cyes / and not by the only wurde of God. Suche are they which
now have the doynges in these present controversyes / and
oppresse the most manifest verite. God amende it.

I write not this rude treatise / for that I woulde receyve
praise therof / but that I wolde God to have all the prayse Prayse
/ which hath bene a moste wonderfull wurker therin. For I 246
am but a clodde of coruption / felinge in my self as of my
self / nothinge els but sinne and wickednesse. I have done
it also / to declare my most earnest rejoice in the same God
/ which by grace hath called me by persecucion hath tried Gods
me / and of favour / benivolence and mercye / hath most wurke
wonderfully delivered me. Lete hym that rejoyceth (saith S.
Paule) rejoyce in the Lorde. For he that prayseth him selfe /
is not allowed / but he whom the Lorde prayseth (2 Corint. 254
10). Moreover I have done it / for that my persecuted bretherne Brether
might in lyke maner have their rejoyce in that heavenly Lorde ne

/ whiche mightelye hath wrought in them their salvacion
/ by his graciouse callinge of them from wicked Papisme to
fol. 8 [Aviii] true christianyte / and now tryeth their paciences by con-
Delyve tynuall afflictions / and finally will delyver them / eyther
raunce from tyrannouse molestacions / as he hath done me / eyther
els into martirdome for his truthes sake. For God wil be
knowne by none other doctryne / than he hath sent hyther by
hys sonne / whom he so earnestly commaun-
265   ded to be heard. He will also be worshipped by those rules only / whom he hath
to hys church proponed by hys pro-
Prayer   phetes and apostles. I besiche that
everlastyng God for hys dere
270   sonnes sake / in the holy Ghost
to rule us / and alwayes
to augment and preser-
ve hys true churche
confessing his on-
275   ly name.
Amen.

I called uppon the Lorde in my trouble /
and the Lorde hearde me at large. The
Lorde is my helper / I wyll not feare
280   what man doeth unto me.
Psal. 118.

fol. 8ᵛ [Aviiiᵛ]   **VERITAS DOMINI MA-**
net in aeternum. Psalm 116.

(Device)

285   **NOVIT DOMINUS VIAM**
justorum, & iter impiorum
peribit. Psalm. 1.

¶ VERITAS DOMINI, MA=
net in æternum. Pſalm. 116.

¶ NOVIT DOMINVS VIAM
iuſtorum, & iter impiorum
peribit. Pſalm. 1.

¶ of Johan Bale to
the byshoprycke of Ossorye in
Irelande his harde chaunces therin /
and finall delyveraunce.

IN the olde and newe testament is it not expressed / that
any just or faythfull man ever yet toke upon hym / the Mini-
adminystracyon of the heavenly doctryne / in teachynge the sterie.
true worshippynges of God / and in persuadynge men to repen- 296
taunce or amendement of their former lyfe / without the vocacion and speciall election of God. No truly / Balaam the notable sothsayer coulde neyther curse nor yet blesse / without
Gods permission / as he apertly confessed (Num. 22). And 300
to beginne with the formest examples. Adam our first pro- Adam.
genitour / whiche had receyved most helthsome instructions
of Gods eternall sonne in paradyse / and the fathers him suc-
cedinng in the righteous lyne befor the generall floude / never
had taken that high office upon them / had not he therunto 305
both called them / & alowed them. Noe, Gods true servaunt Noe.
/ at his most graciouse appointement also / by the space
of an c. years & xx. earnestly preached to the people of that
age / exhorting them to cease / from the ab[ho]minacions
than used / as thei wold avoide the universall destruccion   fol. 9ᵛ Biᵛ
which folowed. After the seyd floude / by vertue of the selfe 311
same precepte and autoryte of God / Noe taught the people Noe
/ than growne to an increase againe / by longe continuaunce.

So ded **Melchisedech in Salem, Job in Arabia, Abraham in**
315 **Chaldie, Jacob in Mesopotamy, and Joseph in Aegypte, He-**
lias with the other prophetes in **Israel, Jonas in Ninyve, Daniel**
fathers **in Babylon, Zorobabel in Persie, and Johan Baptist in Jewrye**.
Marke the open places of the scripture / concernyng Vocacion and Election.

320   And as towchyng Christe in our manhode / he was called
of God his eternall father / as was Aaron / to be our everlast-
Jesus. ing preste / accordinge to the ordre of Melchisedech (Hebre.
7). He was also by his owne godly mouthe / to the worlde
declared / that wele beloved sonne of his / in whom he was
325 most highly both pleased & pacifyed. Finally he was by hys
most heavenly ordinaunce / constituted oure universall doc-
A may- tour / and of him commaunded / as a most perfight maistre
stre. / of all men to be most diligently hearde & obeyed. From
the shippe / from the c[u]stomehowse / & from other
330 homely ministerys / called he / not the stought / sturdye
/ & heady sort of men / but the lowly harted / simple / &
fol. 10 Bii beggarly ydiotes. Them he elected most gracyously / &
they not him / to be the ministers of his holy Gospell /
apostles (Johan. 15). Them chose he out from the world / to gyve
335 knowlege of salvacion to hys people / for the remission of
their synnes (Mat. 10, Luce. 2). Those (sayth S. Paule) whom
the Lorde appointed before / those hath he also called / and
those whom he hath called / those hath he lykewise justified
Election. / or made mete for that heavenly offyce (Rom. 8). For how
340 shuld they have preached (sayth he) unlesse they had ben sent
(Rom. 10). Peter was to him an elect apostle / affirminge hys
S. Johan doctrine to be the wurdes of eternall lyfe / (Joan. 6). John was
his derely beloved disciple / & became a most mightie thun-
derer out of the same (Act. 4). Paul was a peculiar chosen ves-
345 sel unto him / to manifest hys name before the Gentyles /
Kynges and chyldren of Israel (Act. 9).

The Idolatour / the tyraunt / and the whoremongar / are
Papys- no mete mynisters for hym / though they be never so gor-
tes. gyously mytered / coped / and typpeted / or never so fynely
350 forced / pylyoned / and scarletted. The deceytfull prophetes
(sayth the Lorde) made spedy haste / but I appoynted them

not. They ranne a great pace / but I sent them not. They
prophecyed fast / but not out of my spret (Hier. 23). To the
wicked doar the Lorde hath spoken it (sayth David) whie doest   David.
thu so unjusttly presume to talke of my righteousnesses /   fol. 10ᵛ Biiᵛ
and with thy polluted mouthe / of my eternall testament /   356
whie makest thu relacion? (Psal. 50). After the Apostles immediatly succeded in the primative churche / **Tymotheus,**
Ignatius, Policarpus, Iren[ae]us, Paphnutius, Athanasius, Lac-   Doct.
tantius, and other true ministers of the Gospell. These loy-   360
tered not in the vineyearde of the lorde / as our ydell masmongers do / but faithfully they laboured in sekinge Gods
glorie / and the sowles helthe of the people. But whan great
Constantine the Emprour had gyven peace to the Christen   Peace.
churche / that all persecucion ceased / than came in   365
ceremonie upon ceremonie / & none ende was of them. Every
yeare entered one poyson or other / as mannes fyckle nature
in this frayle lyfe / is never without vice.

So that s. Augustine in his tyme very muche lamented /   Throl-
that so many supersticions were than crepte in / confessinge   dom.
the servitude of the Christen churche to be more grevouse   371
in those daies / than it was to the people undre Moyses. And
so muche the more he lamented the case / that beinge but
one man / he coulde not reforme it / neither was he able in
everye pointe to resist that evill / beinge with heretykes so   375
sore tossed on every syde. But what wolde he have sayde
if he had seane the abhominable ydolatries of our time   fol. 11 Biii
without nombre? specially the worshippinge of breade and   Augu-
of wyne / which are only the servauntes of our bellies / and   stine.
corrupt in the same / yea / whan they are at the best &   380
holiest. For whan they have done their office / beinge   Breade
sacramentes of Christes bodie and bloude / that is to saye
/ preached the lordes deathe till he come / and declared us
of manie members to be one misticall bodie in Christe / they
ascende not into heaven / but beinge eaten and disgested /   385
they are immediatly resolved into corruption. Yea / Christe   Christe.
sayth / that they descende downe into the bellie / & are cast
out into the draught / (Math. 15) which declareth them un-
mete to be worshipped.

390   This write I / not in unreverencinge the sacrament / but
in detestacion of the abhominable ydolatries / therin most
bestially committed.

And brevely to saye sumwhat of the Christen churche of
England our realme / in those dayes called Britaine / and now named
395 Englande / what originall it had and from whens / what continuaunce / what darkeninges / what decayes / what falle
/ and what rayse againe.

To fatche this thinge from the first foundacion / for that
fol. 11ᵛ Biiiᵛ lande / lyke as for other landes. By the eternall sonne of God
Adam. in Paradyse / receyved Adam the first promise of salvacion
401 in the womans sede. This acknowleged Abel in his first
offeringe up of the firstlinges of his flocke & fatt of the same
beinge so instructed by that religiouse father of his (Gene. 4).
Abel. By faithe in his plentuouse sacrifice (saith s. Paule) ob-
405 teined Abel / witnesse that he was righteouse (Heb. 11). This
with the right invocacion of the name of God taught by Seth
and Enos / was continued by the chosen of that line / to remayne styll in remembraunce to their posteritees / & was
renued after the floude by righteouse Noe / (Gene. 8). To S.
410 Paule also in revelacion / was this misterie shewed / that the
the lambe Gentiles lykewyse were partakers of the promyse / (Ephe. 3).
Wherunto S. Johan sayth / that the lambe was slayne from
the worldes beginninge / (Apo. 13), that is to saye / in promise
/ in faithe / & in misterie of their sacrifices. Applied is it
415 also to those Gentiles / in the seyd Revelacion of S. Johan
(who now amonge other includeth our lande) that they from
gentyls. that time have cryed with a lowde voyce / seinge, Helthe be
to him that sitteth upon the seate of our God / & unto the
lambe (Apo. 7). And therupon Gildas in Excidio Britannie,
420 concludeth / that the inhabitours of our realme / have alwayes had knowlege of God / almost sens the worldes beginninge.

fol. 12 Biv   This rule of sacrifice and invocacion / helde Japheth after
Japhet. the floude also / the father of Europa containinge our lande
425 amonge others / accordinge to the prayer of his righteouse
father Noe / that he mighte dwelle in the tentes of Sem (Gene.
Melchi 9) or in faithe of the promised sede which is Christe (Gala. 3).
sedech. So perfyght was Melchisedech or the forenamed Sem / a

father than of the Gentiles / for that his kinrede (sayth
Paule) is not reckened amonge the tribes / that he toke tithes 430
of Abraham / & blessed him that had the promises (Hebre.
7 et Gene. 14). For so muche as God / (sayth Luther upon
Genesis) established the kingedomes of the Ilandes / whan
they were divided / by the chosen fathers / it semeth wele
that they helde his true worshippinges / received a fore of 435
them. To these holy fathers in the Gentilite for that realme fathers
/ by course succeded / **as Berosus, Plinius, Strabo, Caesar,
& other authors writeth, the Samothees, Sarronites, Druydes,
Bardes, Sybylles, Eubages or Vates, Flamines,** & suche
other / till the comminge of Jesus Gods sonne in the Christe
fleshe. Which all acknowleged but one God / what though 441
it were by the diversite of rytes and doctrines. This have I written here / to declare what churche was in our lande afore
Christes comminge. I speake nothinge of them which folowed
straunge worshippynges or manifeste ydolatryes of the heathen fol. 12ᵛ Bivᵛ
/ as the papistes do in thys age. If it be reasoned / how they papistes
coulde heare? S. Paule answereth it out of David / that the
heavens preached to them / all the worlde hearyng it / if none
had done it els (Rom. 10 et Psal. 19) besyde the lawe of nature / which was also their leader. 450

In the .63. yeare after Christes incarnacion / to resort to Joseph.
my purpose / was Joseph an hebrue and disparsed disciple
thydre sent with his companyons / by Philipp the apostle than
preachynge in Fraunce / as **Freculphus** in the seconde part
of hys Chronycle / **& Isidorus also de vita & obitu sancto-** 455
rum patrum, rehearseth. He publisshed there amonge them
/ that Gospell of salvacion / whiche Christe first of all / &
afterwardes hys Apostles had taught at Jerusalem. Untruly apostles
therfore are we reported of the Italyane writers / and of the
subtylle devysers of sanctes legendes / that we shulde have 460
our first faythe from Rome / and our christen doctryne / from
their unchristen byshoppes. From the schole of Christe hymselfe / have we receyved the documentes of oure fayth. From Hieru-
Jerusalem / & not from Rome / whom both Peter & also salem.
Christe hath called Babylon / for that she so aptely therunto 465
agreeth in ministryng confusion to the world. And this wele fol. 13 [Bv]
accordeth with the wurdes of the prophete / that the lawe

of the Gospell shulde come from Sion / & the wurde of God
s. Paule from Hierusalem (Esa. 2). S. Paule also which had bene
Clau- christenly familiar at Rome / with Claudia Rufina a Britayne
dia. borne / and with Aulus Pudens her husbande / of whome
he maketh mencion (2 Timoth. 4) shulde seme in his owne
persone to have preached in that nacion of ours / by this sainge
of his in the same epistle and chaptre: The lorde assisted me
475 and strengthened me at my first answeringe / that by me the
preachinge shulde be fulfilled to the uttermost / and that all
the Gentiles shulde heare. That clause / all the Gentiles /
Gentiles includeth sumwhat concerninge the Britaines / if they were
than Gentiles / & in the west part of the worlde / as we can
480 saye none other of them.

  Bartholomeus Tridentinus & Petrus Calo reporteth in
Timot. their bokes of the lives of sanctes / that Timothe, S. Paules
disciple / by his preachinge in Britaine / converted kinge Lucius & him baptised / in confirmacion of that is said afore.
485 Nurrished / brought up / & continued was this Brittish
Brita- churche in the doctrine of faithe / without mennes tradicions
nes. / by the wurthie doctours of that age / **Elvanus, Meduinus,**
Melanius, Amphibalus, & suche other like / till the time of
fol. 13ᵛ [Bvᵛ] Diocleciane the tirannouse Emproure. Which by his wicked
490 ministers / made havock of the Christen flocke there / as
testifieth Gildas. Though the kinges of Britaine in that age
Peace. / **Arviragus, Marius, Coillus, Lucius, and Severus,** with others
/ were not all Christened / yet were they no cruell persecuters
of Christes congregacion / that we reade of. In the generall
495 quyetnesse provided to the churche by the forenamed **Con-**
Herety- **stantine, Arrius, Pelagius, Leporius, and one Tymothe,** part-
kes. ly by subtile allegories / and partly by open heresies greatly
Monkes obscured the glory therof. Anon after there folowed a certen
kinde of monkery / with an heape of ceremonies / but yet
500 without blasphemouse supersticions / till Antichrist had
Doct. fashioned them to his execrable use. In that age were **Fastidius,**
Ninianus, Patritius, Bachiarius, Dubricius, Congellus, Ken-
tigernus, Iltutus, David, Daniel, Sampson, Elvodugus,
Asaphus, Gildas, Beulanus, Elbodus, Dionotus, Samuel, Nen-
Helpers **nius,** & a great sort more / by Christen doctrine the up-

holders of the Brittish churche / the cyvyle governours for 506
that time beinge dissolute & carelesse / as the forseyd Gildas very sharply doth laie it to their charge.

Consequently whan the Barbarouse nacions had subdued
the Christen regions of Europa / specially here in this realme fol. 14 [Bvi]
/ the heathnish Saxons the Christen Britaines / for not Saxons.
obeyenge and folowinge Gods wurde that time faithfully
preached, than entered in an other swarme of monkes / muche
wurse than the other. For they had their beginninge of those
solitary bretherne / which had fled to the wildernesse in the 515
tyme of persecucion. These lyke laysye locustes sprange fourth locustes
of the pytt bottomlesse. They served God in lyberte / and were
fedde of their owne true labours. These served Antichrist in
bondage / and devoured up the labours of other. They were
sumwhat ceremoniouse / but these altogyther supersticiouse. 520
Of this lattre swarme / after the first enteraunce **of Augustine** Augusti
the Romish monke, was Egbert, Egwine, Boniface, Wilfride, ne.
Dunstane, Oswolde, Lanfranck, Anselme, & suche other
without nombre / by whom the sincere faithe of the English
churche decayed. These were bytter stingars in Antichristes 525
cause / yea / terrible accusers & supressers of kinges & accusers
of other christen magistrates. These caused the sunne / which
is the clere verite of the lorde / to apere as sacke clothe made
of heare / (Apo. 6) placinge in the rowme therof / their owne Obscu-
fantastical doctrines / vaine tradicions / & supersticiouse rers
ordinaunces. So that they made Gods heavenly wurde / to
seme to the people / darke / rough / harde / & unpleasaunt fol. 14ᵛ [Bviᵛ]
/ for their ydle bellyes sake.

Yet denye I it not / but some godly men were amonge them
in those dayes: **as Beda, Johan of Beverle, Alcuinus, Neotus,** 535
Hucarius, Serlo, Achardus, Ealredus, Alexander Neckam, Doct.
Nigellus, Sevallus, & suche other. Which though they than
erred in many thinges / yet was not their errour of obstinacie
and malice. Than folowed the schole doctours with the .iiii. Fryres.
ordres of frires / very wicked kindes of men / and they with 540
their sophisticall sorceryes / poysened up altogyther / clere-
ly overthrowinge the Christen churche / and setting up in
her place the most filthye sinagoge of Sathan. In that malig-

naunt assemblye / were false wurshippinges commaunded
for Gods holy service / and monstruouse buggery for a
professed virginite / in our consecrate clergye admitted. Thus
were the people nusled up from their yowth in callinge upon
dead men and ymages / the preastes and religiouse in the
549 meane time occupied / in all beastly wurkes of the fleshe.
Registr. I have the registre of the visitacions of the cloysters of Englande / & therfor I knowe it to their confusion. The monkes
afore their time / ded nomore but mixte the Christen religion
fol. 15 [Bvii] with the paganes supersticions / but these fowle lecherouse
locustes have bannished the Christen religion altogyther. They
Mira- have taken upon them a power by vertu of transubstanciacion
cles. / farre above Gods power / as of corruptible creatures to make
Goddes to be wurshipped / bearinge them a broade with Persicall pompes as it were / in their gaddinge & gaglinge processions / fitt for wanton gossippes to shewe their selves in their
560 holy daye apparelinges.

Yet were there alwayes some in that miste of palpable darke-
Good nesse / that smelled out their mischefes / & in part main-
men. tened the syncere doctrine / as Mathew Parys / Oclyf / Wick-
leff / Thorpe / White / Purveye / Pateshulle / Paine / Gow-
565 er / Chaucer / Gascoigne / Ive / & now in our time William Tindale / Johan Frith / Bilneye / Barnes / Lambert /
& a great sort more. Now truly in this lattre age and ende
Mercye of the worlde God shewinge great mercy to his elected heritage
/ hath gathered them togyther from the parels of perdicion
570 / by the voyce of his holye Gospell. Yea / lyke as by Hieremie the prophete before the exile into Babylon / by Johan
Callinge Baptist / Christe / & his Apostles before the destruction
of Hierusalem / and by the Apostles folowers before the
division and first ruyne of the Romish empire / he called his
fol. 15ᵛ [Bviiᵛ] disparsed remnaunt / so doth he now agayne before his gener-
576 all comminge to judgement / [c]all tog[y]ther his churche of
K. Hen- true belevers / by the godly preachers of thys age. That won-
rye. derfull wurke of God / that noble prince Kynge Henrye the
.8. within thys realme by hys royall power assysted / after that
580 he had gyven an overthrowe to the great Golias of Rome /
K. Ed- oure most godly soverayne Kynge Edwarde the .6. for hys tyme
warde. perfourmyng the same.

The fyrst with noble Kynge David / prepared thys buyldynge
of the Lorde / but thys other with the wyse Kynge Salomon
/ to hys power made all thinges very perfyght. And though 585
now after hys death / a Hieroboam paraventure is risen /
which will sett up the golden calves in Samaria / or mayn-
tayne the popysh religyon agayne / in Ymages / Aulters / ydle A good
ceremonyes / and blasphemouse supersticions. Yet doubt I Kynge.
it not / but a faytfull Asa / shall folowe / eyther els a Josaphat 590
/ an Ezechias / or a myghtye Josias / which will dissolve those
ydolatryes agayne. And as concerning the fornamed Kynge Edwarde / I will recite here / what hys wurthinesse ded for me The au
his most unwurthie subject / that I shuld among others be tor.
a collectour [or] a caller togyther of the christen flocke in thys 595
age.

Upon the .15. daye of August / in the yeare from Christes fol. 16 [Bviii]
incarnacion 1552 beynge the first daye of my deliveraunce recover.
/ as God wolde / from a mortall ague / which had holde
me longe afore. In rejoyce that hys Majestie was come in 600
progresse to Southampton / whiche was .5. myle from my
personage of Bysshoppes Stoke / within the same countye,
I toke my horse about .10 of the clocke / for very weaknesse weake.
scant able to sytt hym / & so came thydre. Betwixt .2. & .3.
of the clocke the same daye / I drewe towardes the place 605
where as his Majestie was / and stode in the open strete ryght
against the gallerye. Anon my frinde / Johan Fylpot a gen-
tylman / & one of hys previe chambre / called unto him .2.
more of his companyons / which in moving their heades frendes
towardes me / shewed me most frindely countenaunces. By 610
one of these .3. the Kynge havynge informacion that I was
there in the strete / he marveled therof / for so much as it
had bene tolde hym a lytle afore / that I was bothe dead & K. Ed-
buried. With that hys grace came to the wyndowe / and ear- warde.
nestly behelde me a poore weake creature / as though he had 615
had upon me so symple a subject / an earnest regarde / or
rather a very fatherly care.

In the same very instaunt / as I have bene sens that time fol. 16ᵛ [Bviiiᵛ]
credibly infourmed / his Grace called unto him / the lordes Lordes.
of his most honourable counsell / so manie as were than 620
present / willinge them to appoint me to the bishoprick of

Ossorie in Irelande. Wherunto they all agreably consentinge
/ commaunded the letters of my first callinge therunto / by
and by to be written and sent me. The next daye folowinge
A lettre / which was the xvi. daye of August / the lettre beinge
626 written by B. Hamptone / a clarke of the counsell / they very
favourably subscribed to the same / in maner as herafter
foloweth.

¶The coppie of the seyd lettre.

630   To our very lovinge frende / doctour Bale. After our hartye
commendacions. For as muche as the kinges majestie is minded in consideration of your learninge / wysdome / and other
vertuouse qualityes / to bestowe upon yow the bishoprick of
Ossorie in Irelande / presently voyde / we have thought mete
635 / both to give yow knowledge therof / and therwithall to lete
yow understande / that his majestie wolde ye made your
repayre hyther to the courte / as sone as conveniently ye maye
/ to thende / that if ye be enclined to embrace this charge
/ his highnesse maye at your comminge / gyve suche ordre
fol. 17 Ci for the farther procedinge with yow herin / as shalbe con-
641 venient. And thus we bid yow hartely farewell. From Southampton the xvi. daye of August .1552.
Your lovinge frendes [J.] Winchestre, J. Bedford, H. Suffolke,
W. Northampton, T. Darcy, T. Cheine, Johan Gate, W. Cecill.

645   And to conclude / thus was I called / in a maner from
deathe / to this office without my expectacion or yet knowlege
vocacion. therof. And thus have ye my vocacion to the bishoprick of
Ossorie in Irelande. I passe over my earnest refusall therof /
a moneth after that / in the kinges majesties returne to Win-
650 chestre / where as I alleged (as I than thought) my lawfull
Impedi impedimentes / of povertie / age / and syckenesse / within
mentes. the bishopes howse there / but they were not accepted. Than
resorted I to the court at London within .vi. wekes after / accordinge to the tenure of the forseyd lettre / and within vi.
655 dayes had althinges perfourmed perteininge to my election

and full confirmacion / frely without any maner of charges
or expenses / wherof I muche marveled.

On the .xix. daye of Decembre / I toke my journeye from
Byshops Stoke with my bokes and stuffe towardes Bri-
stowe / where as I tarryed .xxvi. dayes for passage / and diverse times preached in that worshipfull cytie at the instaunt desyre of the cytiezens. Upon the .xxi. daye of January
/ we entred into the shippe / I / my wyfe / & one servaunt. And beinge but .ii. nyghtes and .ii. dayes upon the sea
/ we arryved most prosperously at Waterforde / in the cold-
est time of the yeare / so mercifull was the Lorde unto us.

In beholdynge the face and ordre of that cytie / I see many
abhomynable ydolatryes mainteined by the Epicurysh prestes
/ for their wicked bellies sake. The Communion or Supper
of the Lorde / was there altogyther used lyke a popysh masse
/ with the olde apysh toyes of Antichrist / in bowynges and
beckynges / knelinges and knockinges / the Lordes deathe
after S. Paules doctrine / neyther preached nor yet spoken
of. There wawled they over the dead / with prodigyouse
howlynges and patterynges / as though their sowles had not
bene quyeted in Christe and redemed by hys passion / but
that they must come after and helpe at a pinche with Requiem
Eternam / to delyver them out of helle by their sorowfull sorceryes. Whan I had beholden these heathnysh behavers / I
seyd unto a Senatour of that cytie / that I wele perceyved /
that Christe had there no Bishop / neyther yet the Kynges
Majestie of Englande any faythful officer of the mayer / in
suffering so horryble blasphemies. The next daye after / I rode
towardes Dublyne / & rested the night folowinge in a towne
called Knocktover / in the howse of maister Adam Walshe
/ my generall commissarye for the whole dyocese of Ossorie.

At supper the parish prest / called Syr Philypp / was very
serviceable and in familyar talke described unto me the howse
of the white fryres which sumtyme was in that towne concludinge in the ende / that the last prior therof called Wyllyam
/ was his naturall father. I axed him / if that were in mariage? He made me answere / No. For that was (he sayd) against
his profession. Than counselled I hym / that he never shulde

Frelye.

660

fol. 17ᵛ Ciᵛ

passage.

665

Water-
forde.

670

Idola-
tours.

675

Decei-
uers.

680

fol. 18 Cii

The maier

685

A preste

690

whore- boast of it more. Whie (sayth he) it is an honour in this
dome. lande / to have a spirituall man / as a byshop / an Abbot /
a Monke / a Fryre / or a Prest to father. With that I greatly
marveled / not so much of his unshamefast talke / as I ded
that adultery forbidden of God / & of all honest men de-
699 tested / shulde there have both prayse & preferrement /
dubline thinking in processe / for my part / to refourme it. I came
at the last to Dubline / wher as I founde my companyon maistre Hugh Goodaker the Archebishop of Armach elected / &
mi olde frynde / M. David Coper person of Calan. Much of
fol. 18ᵛ Ciiᵛ the people ded greatly rejoyce of our comminge thidre /
Idola- thinkinge by our preachinges / the popes superstitions wolde
tryes. diminish & the true Christen religion increace.

Upon the purificacion daye of Our Ladye / the lorde chan-
Chaun cellour of Irelande / Sir Thomas Cusake / our speciall good
cellour. lorde and earnest ayder in all our procedinges / appoynted
710 us to be invested or consecrated / as they call it / bi George
the Archebishop of Dublyne / Thomas the Bisshop of Kyl-
dare / & Urbane the Bishop of Duno assis[t]inge him. I will
G. Bro not here describe at large the subtyle conveyaunce of that
wne. greate Epicure the Archebishop / how he went about to diffarre
715 the daye of our consecracion / that he might by that meanes
have prevented me / in takinge up the proxyes of my
bishoprick to his owne glottonouse use / and in so deprivinge
me of more than halfe my lyvynge for that yeare. As we were
Lock comminge fourth / to haue received the imposicion of handes
wode. / accordynge to the ceremonye / Thomas Lockwode (Block-
721 heade he myght wel be called) the deane of the cathedrall
churche there / desired the lord chauncellor very instauntly
/ that he wolde in no wise permyt that observacion to be done
after that boke of consecratinge bishoppes / which was last
A trait. set fourth in Englande by acte of parlement / alleginge that
fol. 19 Ciii it wolde be both an occasion of tumulte / and also that it
was not as yet consented to by acte of their parlement in
Irelande. For whie / he muche feared the newe changed ordre
of the communion therin / to hindre his kychin and bellye.
730 The lorde chauncellour proponed this matter unto us. The
A Beast Archebisshop consented therunto / so ded the other .ii.

bishopppes. Maistre Goodaker wolde gladly it might have bene otherwise / but he wolde not at that time contende there with them.

Whan I see none other waye / I stepped fourth / and sayde, If Englande and Irelande be undre one kinge / they are both bounde to the obedience of one lawe undre him. And as for us / we came hyther as true subjectes of his / sworne to obeye that ordinaunce. It was but a bisshopprick (I sayde) that I came thydre to receive that daye. Which I coulde be better contented to treade under my fote there / than to breake from that promise or othe that I had made. I bad them in the ende / sett all their hartes at rest / for came I ones to the churche of Ossorie / I wolde execute nothinge for my part there / but accordinge to the rules of that lattre boke. With that the lorde chauncellour right honourably commaunded the cere- monie to be done after that boke. Than went the asseheaded deane awaie more than halfe confused. Neyther folowed there any tumulte amonge the people / but every man savinge the prestes / was wele contented. Than went the Archebishop about that observacion / very unsaverly and as one not muche exercised in that kinde of doynge / specially in the administracion of the lordes holy supper. In the ende the lorde chauncellour made to us and to our frendes / a most frendly diner / to save us from excedinge charges / which otherwise we had bene at that daye.

Within .ii. dayes after was I sycke agayn / so egerly / that noman thought I shulde have lyved / which malladie helde me till after Eastre. Yet in the meane tyme / I founde a waye to be brought to Kylkennie / where as I preached every son- daye & holy daye in lent / tyll the sondaye after Eastre was fully past / never felinge any maner of grefe of my syckenesse / for the tyme I was in the pulpet. Wherat many men / and my selfe also greatly mervaled. Neyther had I for all that tyme space / any minde to call for any temporall profites / which was afterwardes to my no small hynderaunce. From that daye of our consecracion / I traded with myselfe / by all possybyl- yte to set fourth that doctrine / which God charged his churche with / ever sens the beginninge. And thought ther-

the autor
736

An othe
741

the boke.

fol. 19ᵛ Ciiiᵛ

A loite-
rer.

755

An ague

760

Gods
wurke.

765

doctrine

fol. 20 Civ with in my minde also / that I had rather that Aethna ded
771 swallowe me up / than to mainteine those wayes in religion
/ which might corrupte the same. For my daily desire is /
in that everlastinge schole / to beholde the eternall sonne
fathers. of God / both here and after this lyfe. And not only to see
775 the fathers / prophetes and Apostles therin / but also for love
of that doctrine / to enjoye their blessid feliship heraffter. And
so muche the rather I traded thus with myselfe / that I see
than the kinges majestie / the ar[c]hebishopp of Canterbury
Helthe. / and the honourable lordes of the counsell / so fervently
780 bent that waye / as to seke the peoples helthe in the same.
I thought it therupon no lesse than my bounde dewtie / to
shewe my selfe faithfull / studiouse / & diligent in that so
chargefull a function.

Two princi My first procedinges in that doinge / were these. I earnest-
ples. ly exhorted the people to repentaunce for sinne / & required
them to give credite to the Gospell of salvacion. To acknowledge & beleve that there was but one God / & him alone
One without any other / sincerely to worship. To confesse one
Christe Christe for an only saver & redemer / & to truste in none
790 other mannis praiers / merites / nor yet deservinges /
but in his alone / for salvacion I treated at large both of the
heavenly & politicall state of the christen churche / & hel-
pars I founde none amonge my prebendaries & clergie / but
fol. 20ᵛ Civᵛ adversaries a great nombre. I preached the Gospell of
obedience the knowledge & right invocacion of God / I mayntened
796 the politicall ordre by doctrine / & moved the commens
alwayes to obeye their magistrates. But whan I ones sought
to distroye the ydolatries / & dissolve the hypocrites yockes
/ than folowed angers / slaunders / conspiricyes / & in the
800 ende the slaughter of men. Much a do I had with the prestes
Idoles. / for that I had sayd amonge other / that the whyte Goddes
of their makinge / such as they offered to the people to be
worshipped / were no Goddes but ydoles / and that their pray-
ers for the dead procured no redempcion to the sowles departed
805 / Redempcion of sowles beinge only in Christe / of Christe
Prea- / & by Christe. I added that their office by Christes strayght
chinge. commaundement / was chifely to preache / and instruct the

people in the doctryne and wayes of God / and not to occupie
so muche of the tyme in chauntynge / pypynge / and
syngynge. 810

Muche were the prestes offended also / for that I had in Wyves
my preachinges / willed them to have wives of their owne
/ & to leave the unshamefast occupienge / of other mennes
wyves / doughters / and servauntes. But heare what answere
they made me alwayes / yea the most viciouse men among 815
them. What shulde we marrie (sayd they) for halfe a yeare / fol. 21 [Cv]
& so loose our livynges. Thinke ye not that these men were Devy-
ghostly inspired? eyther yet had knowledge of some secrete lish.
mischefe wurkinge in Englande? I for my part have not a little sens that time marveled / whan it hath fallen to my 820
remembraunce. Well the truthe is / I coulde never yet by any Adulte-
Godly or honest persuasion / bringe any of them to mariage rers.
/ neither yet cause them whiche were knowne for unsham-
fast whorekepers / to leave that fylthye & abhomynable oc-
cupyenge what though I most earnestly laboured it. But sens 825
that tyme I have consydered by the jugement of the scriptures
/ that the impenytent ydolatour must therwith be also a
fylthie adulterer or most detestable sodomite. It is his just Sodo-
plage (Rom. I). We can not stoppe it. Lyke wyse the dissem- mites.
blinge hipocrite / in contemning Gods truthe / must nedes 830
folowe errours and lyes in the doctrine of devyls (I Timot. 4)
to have in the ende the greatter confusion. Lete him that is
wicked (sayth that Angell to S. Johan) become more wicked / Wicked
and he that is filthie / become more filthye / that hys damnacion maye be the depar / & his sorowes extremer (Apo- 835
ca. 22).

The lord therfor of his mercie / sende discipline with doctrine / into his church. For doctrine without discipline & doctrine
restraint of vices / maketh dissolute hearers. And on the other fol. 21ᵛ [Cvᵛ]
syde / discipline without doctrine / maketh eyther hipocrites Disci-
/ or els desperate doars. I have not written this in disprayse pline.
of all the prestes of Kylkennye or there about. For my hope
is that some of them by thys tyme are fallen to repentaunce
/ though they be not manye. An other thinge was there / that 844
muche had dyspleased the prebendaryes and other prestes. I Prestes

had earnestly / ever sens my first comminge / requyred them
to observe and folowe that only boke of commen prayer /
whych the kynge & hys counsell had that yeare put fourth by
Excuses acte of parlement. But that wolde they at no hande obeye /
850 allegynge for their vayne and ydle excuse / the lewde example
of the Archebysshop of Dublyne / whych was alwayes slacke
in thynges perteyninge to Gods glorie / alleginge also the want
Justices of bokes / and that their owne justices and lawers had not
yet consented therunto. As though it had bene lawfull for their
855 justices to have denyed the same / or as though they had rather
have hanged upon them / than upon the kinges autorite and
commaundement of his counsell.

sermons. In the weke after Eastre / whan I had ones preached .xii.
sermons amonge them / and established the people / as I
860 thought / in the doctrine of repentaunce and necessarie be-
fol. 22 [Cvi] leve of the Gospell in the true worshyppynges of one God our
eternall father & nomore / and in that hope of one redemer
Holmes Jesus Christe and nomore, I departed from Kylkennie to an
Court. other place of myne .v. myles of / called Holmes Court /
865 where as / I remained tyll assension daye. In the meane time
came sorowfull newes unto me that M. Hugh Goodacker the
Archebishop of Armach / that godly preacher and virtuouse
learned man / was poysened at Dubline / by procurement
Poison. of certen prestes of his diocese / for preachinge Gods verite
870 & rebukinge their commen vices. And letters by & by were
directed unto me / by my speciall frindes from thens / to be-
ware of the like in my diocese of Ossorie / which made me
Kilken- paraventure more circumspect than I shulde have bene. Upon
nie. the assencion daye I preached again at Kilkennie likewyse on
875 Trinite Sondaye / & on S.Peters daye at midsomer than
folowinge.

On the xxv daye of July / the prestes were as plesaunt-
ly disposed as might be / and went by heapes from taverne
879 to taverne / to seke the best Rob davie and aqua vite /
A Joie. which are their speciall drinkes there. Thei cawsed all their
cuppes to be filled in / with Gaudeamus in dolio / the misterie therof only knowne to them / and at that time to none
fol. 22ᵛ [Cviᵛ] other els. Which was that Kynge Edwarde was dead / and that

they were in hope to have up their maskynge masses againe.   K. Edward.
As we have in S. Johns Revelacion that they which dwell on
the yearth (as do our earthly minded masmongers) shulde rejoyce and be glad / whan Gods true witnesses were ones taken
awaye / and shulde sende gyftes one to an other for gladnesse   Giftes.
/ because they rebuked them of theyr wycked doynges / (Apo-
ca. xi). For ye must consydre that the prestes are commenly   890
the first that receive suche newes. The next daye folowinge
/ a very wicked justice called Thomas Hothe / with the Lorde
Mountgarret / resorted to the Cathedrall churche / requyr-
ynge to have a Communion / in the honour of S. Anne.   Idolat.
Marke the blasphemouse blyndenesse and wylfull obstinacie   895
of thys beastly papyst. The prestes made hym answere / that
I had forbydden them that celebracion / savynge only upon
the sondayes. As I had in dede / for the abhomynable ydolatries that I had seane therin. I discharge you (sayth he) of obe-   Satan
dience to your Bishop in this point / & commaunde yow   900
to do as ye have done heretofore / which was to make of
Christes holy communion an ydolatrouse masse / & to
suffre it to serve for the dead / cleane contrarye to the Christen
use of the same.   fol. 23 [Cvii]

Thus was the wicked justice / not only a vyolatour of   A trai-
Christes institucion / but also a contempner of his princes   tour.
earnest commaundement / and a provoker of the people by
his ungraciouse example to do the lyke. Thys coulde he do
whith other mischefes more / by his longe beynge there by
a whole monthes space / but for murthers / theftes /   910
ydolatryes / and abhominable whoredomes / wherwith all
that nacion habundeth / for that time he sought no redresse   Wicked
neyther appointed any correction. The prestes thus rejoycing
that the Kinge was dead / & that they had bene that daye
confirmed in their supersticiouse obstinacie / resorted to the   915
forseyd false justice the same night at supper / to gratifye him
with Rob Davye and Aqua vite / for that he had bene so frendly   T. hoth
unto them / & that he might styll continue in the same.
The next daye after was the Ladye Jane Gylforde proclamed
their Quene / with solemnite of processions / bonefyres /   920
and banquettes / the seyd justice / as I was infourmed / sore   Blamed

blamynge me for my absence that daye / for in dede I muche
doubted that matter.

Kearnes So sone as it was there rumoured abrode that the Kynge
925 was departed from this lyfe / the ruffianes of that wilde na-
fol. 23ᵛ [Cviiᵛ] cyon / not only rebelled against the English captaines / as
their lewde custome in suche chaunges hath bene alwayes
/ chefely no English deputye beinge within the lande / but
English also they conspired into the very deathes of so many English
930 men and women / as were left therin alyve: myndinge / as
they than stoughtly boasted it / to have set up a kinge of their
owne. And to cause their wilde people to beare the more hate
to our nacion / very subtilly but yet falsely / they caused it
to be noysed over all / that the yonge Earle of Ormonde /
Ru-
mours. and Barnabe the Barne of Upper Ossories sonne / were both
slaine in the court at London.

Upon this wylye practise of myschefe / they raged without
ordre in all places / and assaulted the English fortes every-
where.

940 And at one of them by a subtyle trayne / they gote out .ix.
of our men and slewe them.

mastres
Kinge. On the .xiii. daye of August / a gentill woman / the wyfe
of Mathew Kinge / havynge a castell not farre of / her
husbande than beinge at London / fledde with her familie
945 and goodes in cartes towardes the forseid Kilkennye / and in
the hygh waye was spoyled of all / to her very petycote / by
Tiraun
tes. the kearnes & galoglasses of the forenamed Barne of Upper
Ossorie Mihell Patricke and of the Lorde Mountgarret / which
fol. 24 [Cviii] ought rather to have defended her. In this outrage had she af-
950 ter longe conflicte with those enemyes .iiii. of her companie
slain, besides other mischefes more.

Marie. On the .xx. daye of August / was the Ladye Marye with
us at Kylkennye proclamed Quene of Englande / Fraunce and
Irelande / with the greatest solempnyte that there coulde be
955 devysed / of processions / musters and disgysinges / all
Compul-
sion the noble captaynes and gentilmen there about beinge present.
What a do I had that daye with the prebendaryes and prestes
abought wearinge the cope / croser / and myter in procession / it were to muche to write.

I tolde them earnestly / whan they wolde have compelled 960
me therunto / that I was not Moyses minister but Christes Gods
/ I desyred them that they wolde not compell me to his denyall wurde.
/ which is (S. Paule sayth) in the repetinge of Moyses
sacramentes & ceremoniall s[c]haddowes (Gal. v). With that
I toke Christes testament in my hande / & went to the mar- 965
ket crosse / the people in great nombre folowinge. There toke
I the .xiii. chap. of S. Paule to the Roma. declaringe to them
brevely / what the autoritie was of the worldly powers
& magistrates, what reverence & obedience were due to ii. mas-
the same. In the meane tyme had the prelates goten .ii. dis- kers.
gysed prestes / one to beare the myter afore me / and an other fol. 24ᵛ [Cviiiᵛ]
the croser / makinge .iii. procession pageauntes of one. The
yonge men in the forenone played a Tragedye of Gods promises
in the olde lawe at the market crosse / with organe plainges 974
and songes very aptely. In the afternone agayne they played Come-
a Commedie of sanct Johan Baptistes preachinges / of Christes dies.
baptisynge and of his temptacion in the wildernesse / to the
small contentacion of the prestes and other papistes there.
   On the thursdaye next folowinge / which was S. Bar- 979
tylmewes Daye / I preached agayne amonge them / bycause Last ser-
the prebendaryes and other prestes there / had made their mon.
boastes / that I shulde be compelled to recante all that I had
preached afore. And as I was entered into the pulpet / I toke
this sainge of S. Paule for my thema, **Non erubesco Evangeli-** 984
um. Virtus enim Dei est, in salutem omni credenti, &c. I am Gospell
not ashamed of the Gospell. And whie? For it is the power of
God into salvacion / to all them that beleve it (Rom. I). Than
declared I unto them / all that I had taught there sens my first
comming thydre / the justice [H]othe beinge present. As that
our God was but one God / & ought alone to be worshipped. Christe
And that our Christe [was but] one Christe / & ought alone 991
to be trusted to for redempcion of sinne. I earnestly charged fol. 25 Di
the people / to rest upon these ii. principles firmely / as upon
the chefe stayes of their salvacion / as they wolde answere it
at the dredefull daye / and not to suffre themselves to be led 995
by a contrariouse doctrine of deceytfull teachers / into any
other beleve from thens fourth. Item concerninge the sacra- Sacra-

ment. ment of Christes bodye and bloude / wherin they had bene
most prodigiously abused / through the unsaciable covetous-
1000 nesse of the prestes, I required them very reverently to take
it / as a sacrament only of Christes deathe / wherby we are
No wor redemed and made innocent membres of hys misticall bodye
ship. / and not to worship it as their God / as they had done / to
the utter derogacion of his heavenly honour. And as I came
1005 in the Usuall prayer / to remembraunce of the dead, I willed
them to gyve harty thankes to God / for their redempcion in
Christe / largely declaringe that the sowles of the righteouse
were in the hande of his mercye without cruell torment (Sap.
Fune- 3) & that the prestes with all their masses & funerall exe-
rals. quies / coulde nothinge adde to their redempcion / if they
1011 had bene otherwise bestowed.

After the prayer / I toke the Gospell of that daye **Beati oculi
qui vident quae vos videtis, &c** (Luce. 10). Wherin I was oc-
fol. 25ᵛ Diᵛ casioned to speake of certen degrees of men / as of kinges
1015 / prophetes / lawers / justiciaryes / & so fourth. As that the
kinges were desierouse to see Christe / the prophetes to en-
brace him / the swellinge lawers to rise up against him and
to tempte him / and the ambiciouse justiciaries to toye with
the woun him and to mocke him; the wounded man to have nede of
ded man. him / the preste to shewe no compassion / the levite to minis-
tre no mercye / and last of all the contemptuouse Samari-
taine to exercise all the offices of pitye / love / benivolence
/ and liberall mercye / upon the same wounded creature; as
to resort to him / favourably to see him / with layser to be-
1025 holde him / to have compassion on hym / to bynde up hys
Jesus. woundes / to poure in oyle and wyne / to sett him on his owne
beaste / to brynge hym to a place of confort / finaly to socour
him and to paye his whole charges. All these matters I declared
there at large / which were now to muche to repete here
1030 againe. The same daye I dined with the mayer of the towne
R. Shea. / whome they name their suffren / called Robert Shea / a man
sober / wise / and godly / which is a rare thinge in that lande.

Dispu- In the ende of our dyner / certen prestes resorted / and be-
tacion. gan very hotely to dispute with me concerninge their pur-
fol. 26 Dii gatorye & suffrages for the dead. And as I had alleged the

scriptures provinge Christes sufficiencie for the sowles dis- 1036
charge afore God / without their dirtie deservinges, they
brought fourth / as semed to them / contrary allegacions /
that there shulde apere no truthe in those scriptures, as S. s. Paule
Paule prophecied of them (Rom. 1.) That suche as they were 1040
/ shulde seke to turne the veryte of God into a lye. And whan
I had ones deprehended them in that theverie / and agreed
both our alleged scriptures / to the mayntenaunce of my first
princyple / to their manifest reproche, I demaunded of them
/ what a Christen mannys office was / whan suche a scrip- 1045
ture was uttered / as neyther man nor angell was able to denie Offyce.
any truthe therof. But they made me none answere. Than sayde
I unto them, Ye have set me fourth a newe lesson / and taught
me this daye / to knowe a good man from an hipocrite / &
to discerne a true Christiane from a wicked papist. The good ii. sortes
man (sayd I) beleveth a truthe in the scriptures / the hipocrit 1051
denieth it / the christian enbraceth it / the papist doubteth
& disputeth against it / as ded that devill in the wildernesse
with Christe / whan he sought by one scripture to confounde
an other. 1055
    The next daye I departed from thens & went home with Holmes
my cumpanye to Holmes Court agayne. court.
    Where as I had knowledge the next daye folowinge / that fol. 26ᵛ Diiᵛ
the prestes of my diocese / specially one Sir Richarde Routhe
/ treasurer of the churche of Kylkennie / and one Sir James 1060
Joys a familiar chaplaine of mine / by the helpe of one Bar- Barna-
nabe Bolgar / my next neibour & my tenaunt at the seyd be Bol-
Holmes Court / had hired certen kearnes of the Lorde Mount- gar.
garret / and of the Barne of Upper Ossorie / whom they knewe
to be most desperate theves and murtherers / to slea me. And 1065
I am in full beleve / that this was not all without their
knowleges also / for so muche as they were so desierouse of
my landes in diverse quarters / and coulde neyther obteine
them by their owne importunate sutes / nor yet by the frende- tirauntes
shipp of others. As for the Lorde Mountgarret / I suspect him 1070
by this: an horse grome of his / with an other of his brechelesse
gallauntes besides / came into my court one daye / and made ii. the-
a stought bragge amonge my servauntes / that he wolde both ves.

steele my horses / as it is there reckened no great faulte to
1075 steele / and also that he wolde have my heade if I came
abroade.

I sent my servaunt unto him / not as one desierouse to be
Malice. revenged / but to knowe what cause his grome had / to uttre
so muche malice. Yea / I afterwarde complayned therof my-
fol. 27 Diii selfe / to his owne persone / & had but a slendre answere
1081 / with no redresse at all. The Barne of Upper Ossorie / moles-
ted my pore tenauntes in the quarter wher as he dwelte / most
A thefe. maliciously / & Barnabe Bolgar maryed his yonge dough-
ter to one of those murtherers / called Grace gracelesse / to
1085 helpe the matter forwarde. For he thought by that meanes to
have the full occupienge of Holmes Court yet ones agayne.
The cler- On the thursdaye after / which was the last daye of Au-
gie. gust / I beinge absent / the clergie of Kylkennie / by procurement of that wicked justice Hothe / blasphemously resumed
1090 agayne the whole papisme / or heape of supersticions of the
bishop of Rome / to the utter contempte of Christe and his
Rebel- holye wurde / of the kinge and counsell of Englande / and
lions. of all Ecclesiasticall and politike ordre / without eyther stat-
ute or yet proclamacion. They ronge all the belles in the
1095 cathedrall minstre and parrish churches / they flonge up their
cappes to the battlement of the great temple / with smylinges
and laughinges most dissolutely / the justice himselfe beinge
therwith offended. They brought fourth their coopes / can-
Procession. delstickes / holy waterstocke / crosse and sensers. They
1100 mustered fourth in generall procession most gorgiously / all
fol. 27ᵛ Diiiᵛ the towne over / with Sancta Maria ora pro nobis / & the
reest of the latine Letanie. They chattered it / they chaunted
it / with great noyse and devocion. They banketted all the
daie after / for that they were delivered from the grace of God
Decey- into a warme sunne. For they maye now from thens fourth
vers. / againe deceive the people as they ded afore tyme / with
their Latine momblinges / and make marchaundice of them
(2 Petre. 2). They maye make the witlesse sort beleve / that
1109 they can make every daye newe goddes of their lyttle whyte
sowles. cakes / & that they can fatche their frindes sowles from
flaminge purgatory / if nede be / with other great miracles els.

They maye now without checke / have other mennes wives
in occupienge / or kepe whores in their chambers / or els whores
playe the buggery knaves / as they have done alwayes / and
be at an uttre defiaunce with mariage / though it be the in- 1115
sticucion of God / honourable / holye / righteouse / and
perfight.

I wryte not this without a cause / for whie / there were Shame
some amonge them / which boasted both of this and muche lesse.
more / to vayne to be tolde. And whan they were demaund- 1120
ed / how they wolde afore God / be discharged, they made
answere / that eare confession was able to burnish them
agayne / and to make them so white as snowe / though they fol. 28 Div
thus offended never so oft. And one of them for example /
was the dronken bishop of Galwaye / which besides these a bishop
uncomly bragges / furiosly boasted in the howse of one Mar- 1126
tine a faithfull Italiane and servaunt to the Earle of Ormonde
/ and in other howses more / that the bishop of Rome was
the heade supreme of the christen churche in earthe / and
shulde so be proclamed in Irelande / the seyd Martin as Gods martin.
true frinde rebukinge him for it. The exercise of this beastly
bishop / is none other but to gadde from towne to towne over Confir
the English part / confirminge yonge children for .ii. pens macion.
a pece / without examinacion of their Christen beleve / contrary to the christen ordinaunces of Englande / and at night 1135
to drinke all at Rob Davye and Aqua vite / like a man. To a dogge
whome for a mocke now of late / a Galoglasse of the lande confir-
brought hys dogge wrapped in a shete with .ii. pens about med.
his necke / to have him confirmed / amonge neybers children. In this he noted this beastly bishop / more fitt to con- 1140
firme dogges / than christen mennes children.

On the frydaye next folowinge / which was the eyt daye v, ser-
of Septembre .v. of my howsholde servauntes / Rytchard vaunts.
Foster a deacon / Rycharde Headley / Johan Cage / an Irish
horsegrome / and a yonge mayde of .xvi. yeares of age / fol. 28ᵛ Divᵛ
went out to make haye abought halfe a myle of / betwixt 1146
.viii. & .ix. of the cloc[k]e / after they had served God accordinge to the daye. And as they were come to the enter- Al slaine
aunce of that medowe / the cruell murtherers / to the nombre

1150 of more than a score / leaped out of their lurkynge busshes
with sweardes and with dartes / and cowardly slewe them
all unarmed & unweaponed / without mercye. This ded they
in their wicked furye / as it was reported / for that they had
Theves watched so long afore / yea / an whole month space they
1155 saye / and sped not of their purpose concerninge me. They
fellonously also robbed me of all my horses / and of all maistre Coopers horses / whiche that tyme sojourned with me
for savegarde of hys lyfe / to the nombre of vii. dryvynge
1159 them afore them. In the after none / abought .iii. of the
Four hon- clocke / the good Suffren of Kylkennye havinge knowledge
dred. therof / resorted to me with an hondred horsemen / & iii.
hondred fotemen / and so with great strengthe brought me
that nyght to the towne / the yonge men syngynge psalmes
and other godly songes all the waye / in rejoyce of my
1165 deliveraunce.
Kilken-   As we were come to the towne / the people in great nombre
nie. stode on both sydes of the waye both within the gates and
fol. 29 [Dv] without / with candels lyght in their handes / shoughting
out prayses to God for deliverynge me from the handes of those
1170 murtherers. The prestes the next daye to colour their
myschefe / caused it to be noysed all the contray over / that
it was by the hande of God that my servauntes were slayne
A colour / for that they had broken (they sayde) the great holye daye
of our Ladyes nativite. But I wolde fayne knowe / what holy
1175 dayes those bloudthurstye hypocrites / and malyciouse murtherers kepte / which had hyred those cruel kearnes to do
Hipocri that myschefe? O abhomynable traytours / both to God and
tes. to all godly ordre. Ye here commende murther / undre a
colour of false religyon / to hyde your owne myschefes to the
1180 eyes of the people / but the eyes of God ye can not de-
ceyve. Youre horrible slaughter must now be Gods doinge
/ and yet was it the devyll that sett ye a wurke. Ye prate here
of the observacion of the holi daye / which never yet kepte
1184 the holy daye as it shulde be kepte. For ye never yet preached
Decey the wurde of God truly / neither mynystred the sacramentes
vers. ryghtly / neyther yet taught the people to honour God purely / and to kepe his commaundementes inviolably / which
are the only kepinges of the holy dayes.

But on those dayes more than on any other / ye pampre fol. 29ᵛ [Dvᵛ]
them up in all supersticions / false worshippynges / and ydola-
ydolatryes / to the utter defilynge both of the dayes and of tryes.
them. Ye are much offended that a good wurke shulde be done 1192
on the sabboth daye / as were your forefathers the Pharisees
/ but with whoredome / ydolatrye / dronkennesse / and blasphe-
slaughter of men / ye are nothinge at all offended / but wyck- mors.
edly ye do mainteine them / as I am able to prove by a 1196
thousande of your lewde examples. The nativite of our Ladye
/ was at that daye a feast abrogated / by autorite of a Christen
Kynge and his whole parlement / and yet you saye / the holy
daye is broken / whan it is no holy daye at all / but as all Holy
other dayes are holye to them only whiche are holy through dayes.
their true obedience to Gods most holy wurde. Ye had kepte
the daye much holyar in my oppinyon if ye had in the feare
of God obeyd the commaundement of your christen Kynge.
Where as in disobeynge the same / ye have resisted the holy 1205
ordinaunce of God for a supersticyon / procuringe therby to
your selves damnacion (Roma. 1). Christe our heavenly mais- christes
tre and redemer / was wele contented that his most holy nativ- nativite
ite gave place to an heathnysh Emprours obedience (Luc. 2).
And yow disda[y]ne[d] that daye to obeye a most christen fol. 30 [Dvi]
kynge / counsell / & parlement / & yet ye are not ashamed 1211
to boast it / that ye kepte the daie holye. O right Antichristes. On the daye next folowinge which was saturdaye tresurer
/ in the afternone the forseid treasurer a man unlearned and
therwith an outragiouse whorekepar / resorted to me with 1215
a nombre of prestes / to tempte me like as Sathan ded
Christe in the wildernesse / saving that Sathan to Christe
offered stones / & that temptinge treasurer both apples &
wyne. And as they had than compassed me in rounde about tempta
/ the seid treasurer proponed unto me / that they were all cion.
fully minded to have solempne exequies for kynge Edwarde 1221
lately departed / lyke as the quenes highnesse had had them
in Englande. I axed them / how that was? They made me answere / with a Requiem masse & Dirige. Than axed I of
them agayne / who shulde singe that masse? And they an- a masse.
swered me / that it was my bounde dewtie to do it / beinge 1226
their byshop. Than sayde I unto them, Massinge is an office

appointed of that Antichriste the bishopp of Rome / to whome
To prea che. I owe no obedience / neither will I owe him any so longe
as [I] shall lyve. But if ye wyll have me there / to do that
1231 office / which Christe the sonne of God hath earnestly com-
fol. 30ᵛ [Dviᵛ] maunded / whych is to preache hys holy Gospell / I will do
it with all my harte.

Requiem.   No sayde they / we will have a solempne masse / for so
1235 had the Quene. By my trouth sayde I / than muste ye go seke
out some other chaplayne. For truly of all generacions I am
Massin ge. no massemongar. For of all occupacions me thinke / it is most
folish. For there standeth the preste disgysed / lyke one that
wolde shewe some conveyaunce or juglyng playe. He turneth
1240 his back to the people / and telleth a tale to the walle in a
Toyes. foren language. If he turne his face to them / it is eyther to
receive the offering / eyther to desyre them to give him a good
wurde / with Orate pro me fratres for he is a poore brother
of theirs / eyther to byd them God spede / with Dominus
1245 vobiscum / for they get no part of his banket / eyther els to
blesse them with the bottom of the cuppe / with Benedictio
Blessin ges. Dei / whan all the brekefast is done. And of these feates (sayd
I) can I now lyttle skille. With that the Treasurer beynge in
hys fustene fumes / stoughtely demaunded a determinate an-
1250 swere / as though he came not thydre without autorite. Than
suspected I somwhat the wickednesse of justice Hothe and
Justice Hothe. such other. Notwithstandinge I axed him ones again / what
profyght he thought the Kynges sowle to have of those funer-
fol. 31 [Dvii] all exequies? Than answered one of the prestes / that God
1255 knewe wel inough what he had to do. Yet you must appoint
him? sayde I.

If these youre suffrages be a waye for him to heaven / &
To bla- me. that he can not go thydre without them / ye are muche to
blame / that ye have diffarred them so longe. Ye had (sayd
1260 I) a commaundement the last saterdaye / of the justice Hothe
/ to have solempnised them that nyght and the next daye after. But the devyll which that daye daunsed at Thomas towne
(for they had a procession with pageauntes) and the aqua vite
procession. & Rob Davie withall / wolde not suffre ye than to do them.
1265 I desire yow / considering that the last sondaye ye differred

them to see the devill daunce at Thomas towne / that ye will
also this sondaie differre them / tyll suche tyme as I sende
to the Quenes commissioners at Dublyne / to knowe how Commis
to be discharged of the othe which I made to the Kynge and siones.
hys counsell for abolyshement of that popish masse. For I am 1270
loth to incurre the daunger of perjurie. With that after a fewe
wurdes more / they semed content / and so departed. The
next daye came thydre a proclamacion / that they which wolde Procla
heare masses / shulde be suffered so to do and they that wolde macion.
not / shulde not t[h]erunto be compelled. 1275

Thus was that buyldynge clearly overthroowne / and that fol. 31ᵛ [Dviiᵛ]
practyse of blasphemye wolde not take at that tyme / as God
wolde.

And as I had continued there certen dayes / I chaunced Mutte-
to heare of manye secrete mutteringes / that the prestes ringes.
wolde not so leave me / but were styll conspiringe my deathe. 1281
It was also noysed abroad / by the bishop of Galwaye and
others / that the Antichrist of Rome / shulde be taken agayne
for the supreme heade of the churche of Irelande. And to a chaunge.
declare a contemptuouse chaunge from religion to supersti- 1285
cion againe / the prestes had sodainly set up the aulters and
ymages in the cathedrall churche. Beholdinge therfor so many
inconveniences to ensewe / and so many daungers towarde
/ havinge also (which was worst of all) no English deputie deputie
or governour within the lande to complaine to for remedie 1290
/ I shoke the dust of my fete against those wicked colligyners
and prestes accordinge to Christes commaundement / (Math.
10) that it might stande against them as a witnesse at the
daye of judgement. The next daye early in the morninge by To Le-
helpe of frendes / I convayed my selfe awaye to the castell chlin.
of Lechline / and so fourth to the cytie of Dubline / where
as I for a certen time amonge frendes remayned.

As the Epicurouse archebishop / had knowlege of my fol. 32 [Dviii]
beinge there / he made boast upon his ale benche with the olde Ge
cuppe in his hande / as I hearde the tale tolde / that I shulde orge.
for no mannis pleasure / preache in that cytie of his. But this 1301
neded not. For I thought nothinge lesse at that time / than
to poure out the preciouse pearles of the Gospell afore so brock-

a papist ish a swine as he was / becomminge than of a dissem-
1305 blinge proselite / a very perniciouse papist. And as towchinge
learninge / wherof he muche boasted amonge his cuppes /
I knowe none that he hath so perfightly exercised / as he hath
ii. ser- the knowne practises of Sardinapalus. For his preachinges
mons twise in the yeare / of the plough man in winter / by Exit
1310 qui seminat / & of the shepeherde in somer / by Ego sum
pastor bonus / are now so wele knowne by rott of every gos-
sipp in Dubline that afore he commeth up into the pulpet /
they can tell his sermon. And as for his wife / if the mariage
olde shif of prestes endureth not / he hath already provided his olde
te. shifte of conveyaunce / by one of his servauntes. But I wolde
1316 wishe that amonge other studies / he remembred olde De-
bethes at London for surgerie. For ywys there is yet some
moneie to be paied, and an Irish hobby also by promise.

About thre yeares a go / he made interpellacyon to the Kynge
fol. 32ᵛ [Dviiiᵛ] in hys lente sermon / for his daughter Irelande / but now he
Daugh commaundeth her to go a whoringe againe / and to folowe
ter. the same devyll that she folowed afore. For that he ded than /
was but only to serve the time. He neded lyttle than / to have
Accusa- accused Sir Antony Sellenger of treason / if ye marke him wele
cion. now / but that he thought by suche conveyaunce to winne
1326 estimacion / and to obtayne the hygh primacie of Irelande
from the archebisshoprycke of Armach / as he ded in dede.
Full wele bestowed. Suche dissemblinge gluttons / and
swynysh papistes / are a sore plage to that lande / which for
Belli- their wicked bellyes / make the people beleve / that sower
gods. is swete and darkenesse lighte / with their aulters / masses
/ & ymages. And that causeth me to write this to his shame.
The salte (sayth Christe) that is become unsaverie / is from
thens fourth good for nothinge / but to be cast out at the dores
1335 / and troden undre mennes fete / (Math. 5). After certen dayes
/ within my hostes howse / a yonge man of Estsexe called
Tho- Thomas / was comminge and goynge / which for his maisters
mas affayres into Scotlande / had hyred a small shippe / there
called a pyckarde.
1340 I rejoyced at the chaunce / as one that had founde great
threasure / and thought it a thinge provided of God / for my

savegarde and deliveraunce at that present. Anon I covenaunt-
ed with him / to paye the halfe charges of that shippe / that
I might passe thydre with him / and delivered to him out
of hande the more part therof.

    I thought at all tymes by him / and by an other whome
I there had also hearde of / havinge their continuall occu-
pyenges thydre / to have from tyme to tyme knowlege of the
deputyes comminge over into Irelande / and so to resort againe
to myne owne / in case all thinges were to my minde.
As that the tirannouse bishop of Rome had not his primacye
and olde doynges there againe / as it had bene boasted he
shulde / and that the christen religion gave not place to
blasphemouse papistrie. And as he and I were togyther in the
shippe / there tarrienge upon the tyde for passage / an Irishe
pirate / yea / rather a cruell tiraunte of helle / called Walter
/ beinge Pylate as they call them / or loades man in a flem-
mish shippe of warre / made the covetouse Captaine therof
to beleve that I was a frenche man / and that I had about me
innumerable treasure. The Captaine hearinge of this /
with an excedinge fearcenesse invaded our poore shippe / and
removed both the yonge man Thomas and me from thens
into his great shippe of warre. Where as he searched us both
to the very skinnes / and toke from us al that we had in
moneye / bokes / and apparell. He toke also from the maistre of our pickarde or lyttle shippe .v. pounde / which I and
the seyd Thomas had given to him in part of payment / with
all his beere and vitayles / notwithstandinge that he perfightly
knewe us to be English men / & no frenche men.

    In the ende I loked fourth of the Captaines cabyne / and
behelde a fayre howse / as it had bene a mile from us / and
axed of the yonge man / whose howse that was? He made
me answere / that it was the howse of one maistre Parker /
the searcher there. I instauntly desired of the Captayne to be
delivered to him / but in no wise wolde he graunt it. I
required anon after / as I behelde a farre of / the citye of Dubline / to be brought thydre for my honest tryall (for they had
accused me of treason) but it might not be allowed. The next
daye after / we came into the haven of Waterforde / where

fol. 33 Ei

Cove-
naunt.

1345

To kno
we.

1350

Papi-
strie.

1356

Captai-
ne.

fol. 33ᵛ Eiᵛ

roberie.

1366

a howse

1371

1375

dubline

Halfe seas.

as also for my tryall / I desired to go a lande / but in no wyse wolde it be graunted. After that we passed more than the halfe seas over / towardes Cornewale / and were driven backe againe with so fearce and terrible a tempest / that the whole seas to our syght and felinge / went over us. And as we were come yet ones agayne into the haven of Waterforde / I sayde unto the Captayne, God hath with violence brought us hyther againe (I perceyve it) that I shulde trye my innocencye. I desyre yow (sayd I) as I have done hertofore / to deliver me into the cytie of Waterforde / where as I am wele knowne. He refused utterly so to do / and after certen other talke / he desyred me to content myselfe / & I shulde (he sayde) in the shippe / have althinges to my mynde. Whie (sayde I) ye go not my waye / neither is it fitt for me to seke for pryses and to go a roavinge as yow do / but to sattle my selfe sumwhere.

  Sens ye came to our shyppe (sayde he) I hearde yow wishe yourselfe in Duchelande / and I promise yow / we will honestly brynge yow thydre / and not longe tarry by the waye. My chaunce was in dede / to fynde there amonge them / an Hollander / called Leonarde / which knewe me in Nortwyck / with maistre Johan Sartorius. To him in familiar talke / I had wished myselfe there at that present. But how will ye leade me (sayde I to the Captaine) as ye have done hytherto / like a captyve prisoner / or lyke a free passenger? No / sayde he / I take ye now for no prisoner / but for a man of worshipp / and for a most honest passenger / and so will I deliver yow there. But all this time he had my moneie in his owne kepinge. Within .ii. dayes after / we were driven into S. Ives in Cornewale / by extremite of wether. Where as the forseid wicked pyrate Walter / get him a lande afore us / so fast as ever he coulde / & accused me there for an haynouse traitour / yea / for suche a one / as for that cause had fledde out of Irelande.

  And to bringe his wicked purpose to passe / of winninge sumwhat by me / for he thought than to have halfe my moneye which was in the Captaines handes / he fatched thidre one Downinges from .vii. myles of / by the coun-

1384
fol. 34 Eii
Water-
forde.

1390
Frende-
shippe.

1395
Duche-
lande.

1400
A wishe

1405
fol. 34ᵛ Eiiᵛ
moneye

Accusa-
cion.

1415
Downin
ges.

sell of the mariners of that towne / which was noysed to be
the most cruell termagaunt of that shire / yea / suche a one
as had bene a begynnar of the last commocion there / both 1420
to examine me & apprehende me.

And as I was commen to that examinacion before one of Exami-
the baylyfes / the constables / and other officers / I desired ned.
the seyd balyfe / apearinge to me a very sober man / as he
was in dede / to axe of the seyd Walter / how longe he had Walter
knowne me / and what treason I had done sens that tyme 1426
of his knowlege? He answered / that he never sawe me /
neyther yet had hearde of me / afore I came into that shippe
of warre a iiii. or .v. dayes afore. Than sayde the baylife, What   fol. 35 Eiii
treason hast thu knowne by this honest gentelman sens? For 1430
I promise the / he semeth to be an honest man. Marry sayde
he / he wolde have fledde into Scotlande. Whie saith the baylyfe / and knowest thu any impediment / wherfor he ought Scot-
not to have gone into Scotlande? No / sayde the fellawe / but lande.
he was goinge toward Scotlande. If it be a treason (sayth the 1435
baylyfe) to go towardes Scotlande / a man havinge businesse
to do there / it is more than I knewe afore. And truly (sayth
he) than are there manie traitours abroade in the worlde.
Good fellawe (said he) take hede that thy grounde be good The thrust
/ in accusinge this man / els art thu wurthie to suffre due of Ju-
ponnishiment for it. For thu doest it els upon some other das.
affection / than desire of right. With that he stode still / and
was able to saye nothinge / for he was as dronke as an ape
/ in hope of a bone viage.

Than came in the Captaine and his purser / and reviled 1445
the seyd Walter / reportinge him to be a very noughtye fel- Walter
lawe / and a commen dronkarde / and that I was a very honest a dron-
man. For they feared at that tyme / the discharge of my karde.
moneye out of their handes / I offeringe my selfe / for my
tryall against him / to be brought to the sessions / which 1450
were than not farre of. Than sayde the forseid Downinges fol. 35ᵛ Eiiiᵛ
in great displeasure, Gods sowle / what do I here? This is Dow-
but a dronken matter / by the masse. And so went his waye ninges.
in a fume / and for anger wolde not ones drinke with us. So
that I went clere awaye in this prodygiouse conflict. The next 1455

The daye beinge sondaye / I resorted to the temple / to see the
The temple. fashions there. As the peales were all ended / they sange /
mattens / houres / holy water makinge / & masse / all
in Latine. Nothinge was there in English but the poore Letanie
A change / which the preste / a stought sturdie lubber sayde with least
1461 devocion of all / muche of the people lamentinge to beholde
so miserable a mutacion / and saienge, Afore time might we
have learned sumwhat by our comminge to the churche / but
now nothynge at all to our understandynge. Alas / what shall
1465 become of us?

The preste   After dyner / that preste resorted unto us / as bolde as great
Hercules / & after a little talke / fell to flat raylinge of good
Myles Coverdale their bishop after this sort: Where is that
heretyke knave now (sayth he) and other of his companions
A godly / vagabondes / apostates / and runnegates? With other un-
man. comly wurdes. And as I was bent to have made him an answere / a gentilman of the contraie therabout / rubbed me
fol. 36 Eiv on the elbowe / and bad me in mine eare / to lete him alone
/ and I shulde heare wonders. And the seyde Gentilman
1475 brought him into an other talke of olde familiaritees. Wherin he confessed / that he had in one daye / bygetten .ii.
A good mennis wyves / of that parishe with childe / to encreace the
curate. churches profyght in crisyms and offeringes / where as their
husbandes were not able to do it. Yea / mary Sir James sayth
1480 the Gentilman / & ye have done more miracles than that.
A how- Went ye not one daye a fishinge? sayth he. Yes by the masse
sellar of ded I / sayde the preste againe / and made the fyshes more
fyshes. holye than ever the whoresons were afore. For I sent out my
maker amonge them / whome I had that daye receyved at
1485 the aulter. By the masse (quoth he) I was able to holde him
no longar. Sens that daye / I am sure (quoth he) that our
fyshars hath had better lucke / than ever they had afore.

A chur-   Thus when he had raged / by the space of more than an
cheman. houre / the last peale callinge him thens to evensonge / the
1490 Gentilman sayde unto me, These are the ghostly fathers /
which now are permitted to be our spirituall gydes. Are not
A plage we (sayth he) wele apoynted thynke yow? The lorde be mercyfull to us / for it is sure a plage for our unthankefulnesse

whyls we had the truthe. Suche lewde bawdye prestes as this is (sayd he) doth wonderfully now rejoyce / not for any vertue they loke for / but in hope to be mainteined in liberte of all wickednesse / more than of late dayes. Whan supper was done / certen of the mariners resorted to us / declaringe what an uncomly part the preste had played with their pypar / as that he had pyssed in his mouthe / beinge gapinge a slepe in the churche after evensonge. This is the bewteouse face of our Irishe and English churches at this present. The poore people are not taught / but mocked of their mynysters / their servauntes abused / their wives and doughters defyled / and all christen ordre confounded.

As the wether waxed fayre / the Captayne went awaye with the shippe / and was more than ii. miles on his waie / mindinge (as it apeared) to have gone awaye with all that I had / moneye / apparell / and bokes / if the winde had served him wele. The costomers servaunt / an Irishe man also / beinge admonished by his contreyman Walter / of my moneye in the Captaines handes / came to my lodginge in the morninge / and tolde me therof / thinkinge as I had bene in possession therof / if I had come to lande agayne therwith / to have raysed newe rumours upon me / and so to have deprived me therof. For he shewed himselfe very servisable in providinge me a boate / and in bringinge me to the shippe. But whan he ones perceived / that I wolde not demaunde my moneye of the Captaine / and returne agayne with him / though I gave him a crowne for his boate and paynes / yet went he awaye in great displeasure / with no small reproches. And at that present / was the forseid Walter bannished the shippe / for his only troublinge of me / so benivolouse that houre was the Captaine unto me.

The next daye after / I demaunded my moneye of the Captaine / and it was very honestly delivered me / all scysmes / as I thought / pacified. Howbeit that wretched Mammon / most strongely wrought in the unquietouse harte of the Captaine / so that continually after that time / he threttened to sett us on lande / and marvele it was / that he threwe us not both over the borde. Alwayes were we wele contented /

fol. 36ᵛ Eivᵛ

1495

A most vyle knave.

1500

Mockers.

1505

Lyke himself.

1510

an other Judas.

fol. 37 [Ev]

Displeased.

1520

Walter

moneie.

1526

1530

Parell.

to have gone to lande / but yet still he drove it of till we came
into Dover roade / I not understandinge the misterie concerninge the seyd moneye / as that it was in my hande and not
in the Captaines / which marred all the whole matter. In the
meane tyme they went a roavinge by a whole wekes space
and more. And first they toke an Englishe shippe of Totnes
/ goinge towardes Britaine and loaden with tinne / and that
they spoiled both of ware and moneye under the colour of
Frenche mennis goodes. The next daye in the afternone / behelde they .ii. English shippes more / whome they chaced
all that night longe / and the next daye also till .x. of the
clocke / & of them they toke one by reason that his topsaile
brake / and that was a shippe of Lynne. In this had they
nothinge but apples / for he went for his loadinge. After that
traced they the seas over / more than halfe a weke / and
founde none there but their owne contray men / beinge men
of warre and sea robbers as they were.
At the last they came to Dover roade / and there wolde the
Captaine nedes to lande with his purser. My companion Thomas and I / takinge our selfes for free passengers / desyered
to go a lande with them / but that might not be (he sayde)
tyll he had bene there afore. Yes / sayth Thomas / I will go
a lande / if any man go / for I have nothinge to do here. Thu
shalt not go (sayth the Captaine) but I will laye the fast by
the fete / if thu prate any more. With that one Cornelis stode
fourth / and sayde. We are muche to blame / that we have
not dispatched him ere this / and throwne him over the borde.
Than doubted I some mischefe in workinge amonge them.
For one Martin an English pyrate / but yet a frenche man
borne / beinge sumtyme Tompsons man and after that Stran-
guyshes man / and now one and their unthriftie nombre /
had made them beleve / that I was he / which not only had
put downe the masse in Englande / but also I had caused Doctour Gardiner / the bishopp of Winchestre to be kepte so longe
in the tower / & that also I had poysened (whome I loved
& reverenced above all mortall men) the kinge with many
other most prodigiouse lyes.
So went the Captaine & his purser with all these newes

a lande / havinge also with them my bishoppes seale / &
.ii. Epistles sent me from **Conradus Gesnerus**, and **Alexander**
Alesius, with commendacions from **Pellicanus, Pomeranus,**
Philippus Melancthon, Joachimus Camerarius, Mathias
Flacius, and other learned men / desierouse of the English
churches Antiquytees and doctrines. Which letters I had 1575
receyved at Dubline / the daye afore I came to the shippe /
and not yet answered them. These Epistles and seale / with No trea
an other letter sent to me from the counsell of Englande / son.
concerninge my first callinge to that pastorall office / they
had taken out of my male / unknowinge to me. For that they fol. 38ᵛ [Eviᵛ]
had seane the kinges armes in my seale / as the maner is of 1581
byshoppes seales / they layde to my charge the counterfet-
tinge of the kinges seale / upon the .ii. Epistles / heresie .iii. slaun
/ and upon the counsels letter / conspiricie against the Quene ders.
/ so wele were they overseane in that malice for moneye. In 1585
Dover amonge all his cuppes / this captaine discovered these
matters / as what a man he had gotten in the borders of
Irelande / suspiciously passinge over from thens towardes
Scotlande / with all the reest. And as he had perceived some Craftie.
of the hearers desierouse of that praie / he called a great pece 1590
of his tale backe againe / and sayde / that he had sett us a
lande at Southampton / and so letten us go. His minde was
to have solde me / if any man wolde have offered him a good
somme of moneye.

After midnyght he returned agayne to the shippe / pratinge A great
amonge his cumpany / what he had done a lande / and how acte.
he had almost lost all / by his busye talke. But he had hearde
of me (he sayde) muche more than he knewe afore / and he
trusted that I shulde be to him and to all the shippe / a prof-
itable prise. The next daye in the morninge after his first slepe 1600
/ he arose / and with stought countenaunce boasted / that
he wolde strayght to London with his most daungerouse car- fol. 39 [Evii]
ryage / which were we .ii. poore innocent sowles that had To Lon
done yll to noman / savinge that we coulde not beare with don.
the blasphemies of the papistes against God & his Christe. 1605
Muche to and fro was amonge them about that passage. In
the ende they all concluded / that better it was to tarry still

.ii. mas- there with the shippe / whyls one or .ii. of them went to
sengers. the counsell of Englande / in massage and came againe / than
1610 thidre to travaile with shippe and all. To lande goeth the pur-
sar and an other besides / to hyer their horses towardes London, / For mountaines of golde wolde be gotten that wayes
/ they sayde.

Captai-   As I behelde this madnesse / though I little than cared for
ne. my life / yet saide I to the Captaine, Maistre Captaine, what
1616 do yow meane by these straunge turmoilinges? Thinke ye
there is no God? Neither yet a reckeninge to be made at the
lattre daye / of these mad procedinges? The time hath bene
sens our first metinge / that ye have taken me for an honest
1620 passenger / and defended my innocencie against that cruell
Equite. pyrate Walter. How standeth it with equite than / that ye now
proclame me / so haynouse a traitour? I am sure that ye knowe
now nomore by me / than ye ded afore. Your allegacions /
fol. 39ᵛ [Evii ᵛ] that I had put downe the masse / emprisoned Doctour
1625 Gardiner / & poysened the kinge / are most false / as all
of truth the worlde knoweth. My seale & my other letters are plaine
argumentes of my truthe and honest estimacion / and might
be to your confusion / if I chaunced to have righteouse hearers. I praie yow therfor in conscience / that ye tell me / what
1630 evyll ye knowe els by me / that ye make here so terrible
doynges? I can not see / sayth the Captaine / that ye will be
moneye ordered after anye good sort. My only misordre was than /
that my moneye was in my purse / and not in his. Wherunto
I answered / with an hart full of dolour & heavinesse / to
1635 beholde mennis so dampnable practises of mischefe for fylthie
lucres sake.

ordered.   I am contented maistre Captaine (sayd I) to be ordered as
ye will reasonably have me. What will ye gyve than (sayde
the Captaine) to be delivered into Flaunders / and our purser
1640 to be called againe? I answered / that I wolde gyve / as his
selfe wolde with reason and conscience require. If ye had tolde
us so muche yester night (sayde he) this matter had bene at
Zelande. a point / & we by this tyme had bene in Zelande. Than was
all the rable of the shippe / hag / tag / and rag / called to
1645 the reckeninge / rushelinge togyther as they had bene the

cookes of helle / with their great Cerberus / an whole hondred fol. 40 [Eviii]
pounde demaunded for my deliveraunce. In the ende it was
concluded / that no lesse might aswage that Hungrye heate
than fiftie pounde at the least / with this Proviso / that all
the moneie which I had in my purse / with part of my gar- A proviso
mentes also / shulde be out of hande devyded amonge them 1651
and the Captaine / which was .xxi. pounde in the whole.
I instauntly desiered / that it might be receyved in part
[of] payment of the other somme. They cr[y]ed all with A crye.
one voice / Naye / we will none of that. Than I besought them 1655
/ that I might have at the least / an honest porcion therof
/ for payment of my charges / whils I shulde be providinge
/ of so great a raunsome / as they had layde to me.

In fine they assented / that I shulde have .vi. crownes of Allow-
myne owne moneye allowed me / for my costes / tyll I had aunce.
founde out my frindes. Than caused the Captaine a pece of 1661
ordinaunce to be fiered / and a gunne to be lete / to call backe
the purser / and his companion. In whose returne there was
muche to and fro. For some wolde nedes to London / thinkinge
that waye to winne more / than to bringe me into Flaunders. Lucre
And of them which wolde into Flaunders / some wolde to 1666
lande for a barrell of drinke / for in the shippe at that time fol. 40ᵛ [Eviiiᵛ]
/ was neither breade / befe / nor beere. Some feared the
comminge of the mayre and Captayne of the castell / for
searchinge their shippe. So that our Captaine commaunded 1670
them at the last / to hoyse up the sayles and spedily to passe Flaun-
towardes Flaunders. In the meane tyme was I poore sowle com- ders.
pelled / to set my hande to a false bylle of their devisinge /
as that I had hyred their shippe in Irelande for fyftie pounde
/ to bringe me without delaye or tarriaunce into Zelande. 1675
Which I never ded / as the almightie lorde wele knoweth / Compul-
but came from thens with them against my will / and was sion.
tossed to and fro upon the seas / by the space of .xxiiii.
dayes / in folowinge prises / as they call their roberies. And
I was by that time / so full of lyce / as I coulde swarme. 1680

As we came ones thydre / they brought me into the howse Lambert.
of one of the .iiii. owners of the shippe / which was a man
fearinge God / and his wyfe a woman of muche godlynesse

also / which was to me [a] carefull creature / a singular con-
1685 fort provided of God. The next daye were all the .iiii. owners
called to the reckeninge / & a Latyne interpretour wyth
payment. them / to knowe howe / where / and whan / this raunsome
of fiftye pounde shulde be payde? And more than .xxvi.
fol. 41 Fi dayes of layser for the payment therof / might not be graunt-
1690 ed. I desiered to have had liberte to go abroade / to seke my
frindes / but that coulde I not obtaine / though it were in
my former covenaunt / whan the .vi. crownes were delivered
Dronkar me. In the afternone was it noysed abroade, by the dronken
des. mariners all over / that they had brought suche a one with
1695 them out of Irelande / as payed halfe an hondred pounde for
his passage / to the wonderinge of all the towne. So that my
hoste / was fayne to kepe me close in his howse / and to saye
both to the mariners and others / that I was gone to And-
Resort. werpe / the people there resorted so fast to see me. They
1700 reported there also in their dronkennesse / that I was he which
had put downe the masse in Englande / and had throwne Doctour Gardyner into the tower / wyth a great sort of lyes and
slaunders more.

threttes   Thus continued I there / as a prisoner / by the space of
1705 .iii. wekes / sumtyme threttened to be throwne in their commen jayle / sumtyme to be brought afore the magistrates /
sumtyme to be left to the examinacion of the clergie / sumtyme to be sent to London / or els to be delivered to the
Quenes embassadours at Brucels / but alwayes by Gods
fol. 41ᵛ Fiᵛ provysyon I had myne hoste and hostesse to fryndes. And be-
A monke holde a most wondrefull wurke of God. The persone of the
towne / a most cruell monke / a maistre of Lovayne / and
an inquisitour of heretykes / as they call those Rabyes / the
next daye after my comminge / sore syckened / and never
1715 came out of his bedde so longe as I was there / which was
Delibe- greatly marked of some of the inhabitauntes / beinge godly
racion. affected. At the last / in deliberatinge the matter / that they
requyred so muche moneye of me / and wolde not suffre me
to go abroade to seke it / mine hoste bad the Captaine and
1720 mariners considre / how farre they had ronne beyonde the
limites of their commission / in mysusynge the English na-

cion / with whome they had no warre. It maye chaunce herafter (sayth he) depely to be layde to your charges. Therfor   A frende.
by my assent / ye shall agree with this good man for lesse
moneye. Than were they contented to receyve .xxx. pounde   1725
/ as I shulde be able to paye it / and so to discharge me.

Thus hath my lorde God most miraculously delivered me   Delive-
from all these dangerouse parels / and from the gredye   raunce.
mouthes of devourynge lions / into the wurthie lande of Germanye yet ones againe, I hope to the glorie of his most holie   1730
name / everlastinge praise be to him for it. Amen.

Here have ye dere fryndes / a most lyvely and wondrefull   fol. 42 Fii
example of Gods chastenynges / & of his most gracyouse   Gods
delyveraunces agayne. For no chosen chylde receyveth he to   wurke.
enherytaunce / without muche correction (Hebre. 12). The   1735
mercyfull lorde throweth downe into helle / and bringeth from
thens agayne (1 Reg. 2). Though Sathan be suffred as whete
to syfte us for a time / yet faileth not our faithe through
Christes ayde / but that we are at all times readye / to con-
firme the faythe of our weake bretherne / (Luce. 22). I thought   Faythe.
my selfe now of late / for the cares of this lyfe / wele sat-   1741
teled in the bishoprycke of Ossorye in Ireland / and also wele
quieted in the peceable possession of that pleasaunt Euphrates
/ I confesse it. But the lorde of his mercye / wolde   Of mer
not there leave me / what though for the small tyme / I was   cye.
in his vyneyearde / not all an ydell wurkeman / but he hath   1746
provyded me (I perceyve it) to taste of a farre other cuppe.

By vyolence hath he yet ones agayne / as ye in this treatise have redde here / driven me out of that gloryouse Babylon / that I shulde not taste to muche of her wanton pleasures.   Babilon
But with his most derely beloved disciples / to have my in-   1751
warde rejoyce in the crosse of his sonne Jesus Christe. The   fol. 42ᵛ Fiiᵛ
glorie of whose churche / I see it wele / standeth not in the
harmoniouse sounde of belles and organes / nor yet in the
glitterynge of miters and coopes / neither in the shyninge of   Wares
gylte ymages and lyghtes / as the blinde bludderinge papistes   1756
do judge it / but in continuall labours and dayly afflyctions
for his names sake. God at this present / in Englande hath
his fanne in hande / and after his great harvest there / is now   harvest.

1760 syftinge the corne from the chaffe / blessed shall they be /
which persever in faythe to the ende. In case without
doubt / is Englande now / as was Jewrye / after the heavenly doctryne was there plentuously sowne by Christe
and by his Apostles / the true ministers of

Prea-
chers.
his wurde beinge partly enprisoned and
partly dispersed / as they were. God of
his great mercye preserve it from that
plage of destruction / which not only
Hierusalem but also that whole lan-

1770 de tasted / for their wylfull
contempte / of that
massage of their
salvacyon.
Amen.

I **Wryte this unto the / thu sorowfull** churche of Englande
/ that in the middes of thy afflictions thu shuldest not   1776
despayre. Beholde how gracyously / yea / if I may so speake it   The autor.
/ how miraculously and gloriously / the heavenly lorde hath
delivered me / his most unworthie servaunt of all men / and
an excedinge great sinner. He called me of grace to that office   1780
in his vyneyarde / by sore persecucions he proved me of love
/ and at the lattre of mercye & goodnesse he preserved me   Of mer
from the deadly furye of most fearce enemies. Thy callinge   cye.
to the Gospell is not unknowne to the / thu carefull congregacion. Now suffrest thu persecucions diversly / for not   1785
regardinge the time of thy visitacion. Repent yet in the ende
/ and doubtlesse thu shalt have a most prosperouse delyveraunce. They are no noble men / that do vexe the at this
present. They are but pilde peltinge prestes / knightes of the   Repent.
dongehill / though they be sir Swepestretes / maistre doc-   1790
tours / and lorde bishoppes. Loke upon their faces / though
thu measure not them by their frutes / & thu shalt sone
knowe their vertues. They are fierye / hawtie / and lecherouse as gootes / the chastest amonge them. But that   prestes.
shall other mennis wyves knowe / & not thu. A wele   1795
papped Pygion of Paules / is wholsome (they saye) for a tip-
petted gentilman of the popes spialte / in a darke eveninge
/ to coole the contagiouse heates of a coltish confessour.
     No noble men are they / which trouble the in this age /
as I tolde the afore. For true nobylite never yet hated the   1800
truthe of God / but hath advaunced it by all ages. Examples   nobilite
we have in **Adam, Noe, Abraham, Moyses, David, Josias,**
Nycodeme, Joseph, Kynge Lucius, Constantine, Justinyane,
Theodosius, kinge Arthour, Alphrede, Ethelstane, Henry the
seconde, Edwarde the thirde and now last of all that virgine   1805
Kynge Edwarde the .vi. which never was defyled with the   K. Ed-
popes ydolatryes. Immortall fame and note of renowme /   ward.
remayneth yet to them for it. Suche men (sayth the lorde)
as worshipp me / will I make worshipfull / and they that
despise me / shall become ignoble or wretched (i Reg. 2).   1810
These will not take awaye the keye of knowledge from Gods
people / as do the hypocrites / (Math. 23) and as the wicked   Noble
lawers do also / (Luce. 11) wo to them for it. But as the noble   men.

David requireth / they will open the gates that the kinge of
glorie maie entre. Open the gates (sayth he) O ye noble men
/ lete the everlastinge dores be opened / that the kinge of
glorie maye come in / (Psalm. 24).

If any be wicked in this behalfe / which beare the name
of noble men and women, lete them wele weygh with themselves / how Pharo / Antiochus / Herode / and suche other
/ whome God by princely autorite had made noble / by only
tirannie against his manifest truthe / are now become more
vile, than any kichine slave or yet lazar. **Foelix** (sayth Horace)
quem faciunt aliena pericula cautum: Happie is he / whome
an other mannis misfortune maketh wyse.

Over the now triumpheth the bishoppes / the pharisees /
the prestes / and the covetouse lawers. At thy late soden fall
/ rejoyceth the hypocrites / the epicures / the ydolatours /
and the wicked papistes. What shall I saye more? **Johan Baptist** is now derided in the prison. **Jesus** the sonne of God is
grenned at upon the crosse. **Paule** now in **Athens** is hyssed
at. The poore **Apostles** are sliely laughed to scorne. Naye / shall
I yet saye more? **Mycheas** is smitten on the face / whils
Sedechias plaieth the false harlot (2 **Parali.** 18). **Helias** is driven
into the wildernesse / whils Baals chaplaines are banketinge
amonge ladies (3 Reg. 18). **Esaye** is contempned / whils the
prestes are given to ydolatrie and dronkennesse / **(Esa. 28). Hieremie** is sore afflicted / whils Semeias perverteth the truthe
of the lorde (**Hiere.** 29). **Daniel** is throwne into the lyons
denne / whils mischefes are in wurkinge amonge the
wicked (**Dan.** 6). **Peter** is accused of the bishoppes wenche
/ whils Cayphas sitteth in consistorie, condempninge the innocent / (**Math.** 26). **Steven** is called to a reckenninge / whils
the prestes and wicked lawers are bannishinge the Gospell /
(**Acto.** 6). **Antipas** (they saye) is now slaine at **Pergamos**,
whils Simon Magus triumpheth in Samaria / (**Apo.** 2). And
Johan Zebede is sent into **Pathmos**, whils **Cerinthus,
Menander,** and **Hebion** playe the heretike knaves at home /
(**Apo.** 1). Well / lete them plye it a pace. It maye chaunce to
cost theyr poluted Hierusalem a fowle overthrowe / for so per-
secutynge the servauntes of God / in her whoredome / (Esa.

1815
fol. 44 Fiv
open/open
1820

Tirannie

1825

Lawers
1830

Prea-
chers.
1836

fol. 44ᵛ Fivᵛ
Perver
ters.

1844
prestes.

1849
Spiri-
tualte.

1), yea / servauntes I saye, for they served faithfully in the
paynefull office of the Gospell.

Those ydell mercenaries / not only loyter in the vineyarde
/ but also like cruell wolves they ravishe and destroye / (Joan.   1855
10). Of that which God hath expressely forbidden / they make   wolves
now a solempne religion / both in the refusall of marryage
/ and in the prodygyouse veneracyon of ymages / sainge yea
to his naye / and naye to his yea. God sayth / it is not good
for man to be alone /without an helpe / which is a wife in   1860
marriage / (Gene. 2). They saye contrariously / that it is more   fol. 45 [Fv]
than good / for it is holye / religiouse / and prestlike / to   A wyfe.
have no wives of their owne / what so ever they have of other
mennis / besides buggery boyes. I trowe Doctour Weston will
saye none other at this daye / what though not longe a go   weston.
he brent a beggar in S. Botolphes parishe without bishops gate,   1866
gevinge her no wurse than he had received afore of that
religiouse occupienge. The same Weston proponed to an other
woman of his parrish / which was a mannis wife / that her
husbande beinge a slepe / she might lawfully occupie with   1870
him / by vertue of this texte / **Mulier dormiente viro, a lege**   Occupi-
soluta est (1 Cor. 7). If this scripture were not religiously ap-   enge.
plyed / lete them tell me which knowe the right handelinge
of them. Whils this priapustick prelate / is prolocutour in
the convocacion howse / I trust we shall lacke no good lawes for   1875
religion, the man is so religiouse. O abhominacion. Though   priapus
they now are busily spisinge and paintinge of a toorde (their
ydolatrouse masse) yet will a toorde be but a stinkinge toorde
/ both in smelle and syght / pepper him and bawme him
/ garnish him and gilde him as wele as they can / all the packe   1880
of them. To conclude. Now are their most filthie buggeries
in the darke / with their other prodigiouse whoredomes,   fol. 45ᵛ [Fvᵛ]
holden a most pure state of livinge, holy marriage disgraced   Celiba-
/ contempned / and bannished.   tus.

God sayth, Thu shalt make no graven ymage to worshipp.   1885
They saye / ye shal[l] not only make ymages / but ye shall
also gylde them / sense them / worshipp them / and axe helpe   ymages
of them / for whie they are the laye mennis Gospell. In dede
Porphirius that blasphemouse heretike / and troubler of the

1890 Christen churche / as Eusebius reporteth him / was the first
that called them the laye mennis Calender. And though S.
Grego- Gregorie the great / comminge after / confirmed the same
rie. Calender / yet shall it remaine an horrible blasphemie /
bycause God hath in paine of dampnacion forbidden it.
1895 **Epiphanius** that worthie father of the churche / nombreth the
worshippinge of our ladyes ymage amonge heresies. If we be
of his opinion / we must judge yow no lesse than most perniciouse heretikes. Moreover it is now become a religion
Herety- agayne in Englande / to call upon dead men with Sancte Petre
kes. ora pro nobis. This also is fatched from the olde paganes sor-
1901 ceries, for holde hath it none of the scriptures canonicall. How
howlinge and jabberinge in a foren language shulde become
fol. 46 [Fvi] Gods service, that can I not tell. But wele I wote that S.Paules
In La- doctrine doth utterly condempne it / as supersticiouse beg-
tine. gerie / bycause it is but an ydell noise & nothinge to edifica-
1906 cion (1 Cor. 14).

Some men peraventure will marvele / that I utteringe matters of Irelande / shulde omitt in this treatise / to write of
Coyne and lyverie. Which are so cruell pillages & oppres-
Coyne sions of the poore commens there / as are no where els in this
and liverie whole earthe / neither undre wicked Saracene nor yet cruell
Turke / besides all prodigiouse kindes of lecherie and other
abhominacions therin committed. Thre causes there are /
which hath moved me not to expresse them here. One is /
1915 for so muche as they perteine nothinge to the tyttle of this
boke / which all concerneth religion. An other is for that the
3. causes matter is so large / as requireth a muche larger volume.
The thirde cause is / for that I have knowne .ii. worthie
men / whome I will not now name / to have done that thinge
1920 so exactly / as noman / (I suppose) therin can amende them.
But this will I utter brevely / that the Irishe lordes and their
ii. bokes undrecaptaines / supportinge the same / are not only companions with theves / as the prophete reporteth / (Esa. 1) but
also they are their wicked maisters and mainteners. So that
fol. 46ᵛ [Fviᵛ] they both coupled togyther / the murtherer with his mais-
1926 tre / and the thefe with his maintener / leave nothinge un-

devoure behinde then in that fertile region / nomore than ii. sortes
ded the devouringe locustes of Egypte (Exo. 10). Anon after
their harvestes are ended there / the Kearnes, the Galloglasses
/ and the other brechelesse souldiers / with horses and their 1930
horsegromes / sumtyme .iii. waitinge upon one jade / enter
into the villages with muche crueltie and fearcenesse / they
continue there in great ravine and spoyle / and whan they
go thens / they leave nothinge els behinde them for payment villages
/ but lice / lecherye / and intollerable penurie for all the yeare 1935
after. Yet set the rulers therupon a very fayre colour / that
it is for defence of the Englishe pale. I besiche God to sende
suche protection a shorte ende / & their lordes & Captaines also / if they see it not sone amended. For it is the An ende
utter confusyon of that lande / and a mayntenaunce to all 1940
vices.

Thre peoples are in Irelande in these dayes / prestes / lawers / and kearnes / which will not suffre faythe / truthe /
and honestye to dwelle there. And all these have but one God
their Bellye / and glorie in that wicked feate to their shame ii. threes
/ whose ende is dampnacion / (Phil. 3). I speake only of those 1946
which are bredde and borne there / and yet not of them all.
These for the more part / are sworne bretherne togyther in fol. 47 [Fvii]
mischefe / one to maintaine an others maliciouse cause / by
murther previly procured. And to bringe their conceyved wick- 1950
ednesse to passe / they can do great miracles in this age /
by vertue of transubstanciacion belyke / for therin are they previly.
very conninge. For they can very wittely make / of a tame
Irishe a wilde Irishe for nede / so that they shall serve their
turne / so wele as though they were of the wilde Irishe in 1955
dede. Lyke as they ded properly and fynely / in the most
shamefull and cruell slaughter of my .v. servauntes / by the
lorde Mountgarrettes kearnes / and the Barne of upper Ossoryes
farye knightes. By suche fyne conveniaunce of accusinge practyse
the wilde Irishe / and colour of the holy daye broken / as is 1960
written afore / they can alwayes apere to have fayre white
handes / and to be innocent maydes / what murther so ever is
by them committed. But I axe of the prestes / chefely of

Finely. Richarde Routhe the treasurer and of sir James Joys his companion / what they ment by their so oft rydinge to that Barne
of upper Ossorie / whan I was dwellinge at Holmes court?
Whome they neverthelesse to me reported / to be the most
errande thefe and mercilesse murtherer of all the lande. And
what they have ment also / to be so familyar with the furi-
ouse famelye of Mountgarrett? Commenly resortinge in the
endes of all those journayes / to the howse of Barnabe Bolgar. As I suspected the matter than / so have I sens that time
proved it effectually true. Moreover I myght axe of the lawers
/ whie they seke to have so many theves & murtherers
perdoned / specially whan they have slaine English men and
done their robberies within the English pale? But at this time
I leave them / and returne againe to my purpose.

Now must I saye sumwhat to the / thu carefull churche
of Englande / concerninge thy misbehaver against thy most
lovinge Creatour. God chose the for his elect vyneyarde / yea
/ he plenteously pourged and prepared the. But whan thu
shuldest have brought hym fourth frute / for grapes thu gavest
him thornes / (Esa. 7). He loked to have had at thy handes
after the Gospell preachinge there / faythe /knowledge
/feare / love / repentaunce / obedience / true invocacion / &
hartie thankes for his manifolde giftes, with suche other
wholesome frutes of lyfe.

And in stede of them / thu hast brought fourth / ydolatrie
/ blindenesse / impenitencie / frowardnesse / crueltie / pride
/ fornicacion / unclennesse / covetousnesse / ingratefull contempte of the truthe / and hate of the faithfull preachers therof
/ with other sower crabbes of dampnacion.

Thu woldest faine be like the Malignaunt churche of the
papistes / prosperouse and welthye in wordly affaires / and
therwith sumwhat gloriouse. But thy eternall father in heaven
/ will not so have the / but by persecucions transfourmeth
the into the very similitude of his derely beloved sonne / to
whome he hath espowsed the / to reigne with him at the lattre
in eternall glorie.

God hath sufficiently declared in the scriptures / what his
churche is in this worlde. As that it is an afflicted and sorow-

Finely.
1965
fol. 47ᵛ [Fviiᵛ]
double-
nesse.
1974
Lawers
1979
A chur-
che.
1985
Grapes
fol. 48 [Fviii]
1991
thornes
1995
Lyke
Christe
2000

full congregacion / forsaken in a maner / and destitute of all
humaine confort in this lyfe. It maye right wele be compared   The chur-
to a flocke of orphanes / which beinge destitute of father and   che.
mother / are in this worlde subject to manye sorowfull calami-   2005
tees & miseryes. But because that poore churche shulde not
utterly discourage in her extreme adversitees / the sonne of
God hath taken her to his spowse / and hath promised her
protection / helpe and confort / in all her afflictions and parels.
So that she maye at all tymes confort herselfe with this verse   2010
of David / Though my father and mother hath left me / yet   Helpe.
hath the lorde taken me up / for his / (Psalm. 26). In the first
promyse was she taken to grace after transgression / and as-   fol. 48ᵛ [Fviiiᵛ]
sured of delyveraunce from synne / deathe / helle / and the   Confort.
devill. For if God had not most wonderfully collected her   2015
togyther / preserved her / saved her / and defended her / it
had not bene possible for her to have escaped in so horrible
daungers / as were in the universall floude / in the burninge
of Sodome and Gomer / undre the tirannie of Pharao / in   defence.
the journeie through the reade sea / in the captivite of Baby-   2020
lon / and destruction of Jerusalem / and in so manye wonderfull alteracyons and terryble ruynes of the Romane Empyre /
so manye Devyls / Paganes / Mahumetes / Turkes / Jewes /
Epicures / heretykes / popes / byshoppes / monkes / prestes /
and tyrauntes reigninge.   2025
    A perpetuall and unplacable enemye is Sathan / and ever-   Empire
more hath bene / to that poore congregacion / sekinge not
only to disfigure her / but also to spoyle her and destroye her
utterly. Like as it is saied (Gen. 3) that he shulde treade Christe   2029
on the hele. This excedinge great benefight of the goodnesse   Sathan
of God / ought to be remembred / that he after the sinne of
our first parentes / not only received this churche to grace
/ but also hath ever sens / both preserved & defended it. But
alac / great is the untowardnesse & muche is the
hardenesse of mannis harte / that he neglecteth so high a   fol 49 Gi
benefight / as is also the patefaction of Christe in the Gospell   2036
/ by whome we are redemed / and so remayne unthankefull
for the same. A most swete voyce is it unto us / from the sonne
of God Jesus Christe / that he will not leave us as orphanes

2040 / or fatherlesse and motherlesse children without confort, but will come unto us / (Joan. 14). That is / like a gentill and mercifull lorde / he will continually stande by his
churche / assistinge / helpinge / and socouringe it alwaies.
I will be with yow (saith he) to the ende of the worlde /(Math.
2045 28). Lete this be thy confort thu sorowfull churche of Englande,
and staie thy selfe in him which was incarnate / lyved /
wrought / taught / and dyed for thy sinne / yea / he arose
from the deathe and ascended to heaven for thy justificacion
/ (Rom. 4). Cleave thu fast to him / repent thy folyes past
2050 / and take heede to thy doinges from hensfourth. Praye
and fast busily / for this frantyck kinde of Devyls
is never taken awaye / but in prayer and fastinge
(Math. 17). So shalt thu be restored plenteously / & florish in vertues herafter fru-
2055 tefully / to the prayse of one God
eternall. Which liveth and
reigneth worlde with-
out ende. Amen.
𝕱𝕴𝕹𝕴𝕾.

The table of this boke.

𝔉𝔦𝔫𝔦𝔰.   2359

¶Correctyons / where as faultes
hath escaped in the pryntynge.

Fol. 6,   pag. 1, li. 7 at Melita, li. 27 drowned.

           pag. 2, li. 14 at the last

fol. 8,   pag. 2, li. 1 domini

fol. 9,   pag. 1, li. 26 abhominacions   2365

           pag. 2, li. 24 customehowse; Item homely

fol. 10, pag. 2, li. 6 Irenaeus

fol. 13, pag. 1, li. 26 Melanius

fol. 15, pag. 2, li. 2 call togyther

                   li. 26 or a caller   2370

fol. 16, pag. 1, li. 6 Stoke; Item do out the 3 last lines

fol. 24, pag. 2, li. 24 justice Hothe; Item li. 26 Our

                         Christe was but one Christe

fol. 28, pag. 2, li. 3 the clocke

fol. 29, pag. 2, li. 27 disdayned   2375

fol. 33, pag. 1, li. 17 an Irishe pirate

fol. 40, pag. 1, li. 10 in part of payment

fol. 45, pag. 2, li. 5 ye shall

¶Imprinted in Rome / before the castell of
S. Angell / at the signe of S. Peter / in   2380
Decembre / Anno D. 1553.

O lorde thu God of truthe.

J haue hated them ý holde of superſticiouſe va
nitees/ z my truſt hath bene in the.

J will be glad and reiopce in thy mercpe / for
thu haſt conſidered mp trouble / z haſt knows
ne mp ſowle in aduerſitees.

Thu haſt not ſhut me bp into the hande of the
enemie/but haſt ſet mp fete in a large rowme.

Pſalm.xxxi.

Stande bp (O lorde God of hoſtes) thu God
of Jſrael/to bpſet all heathen/and be not mer=
cpfull to them that offende of malpcpouſe wic=
kedneſſe.

Pſalm.lix.

GOD IS

MY HELPER.

O lorde thu God of truthe. [Gviii^v]
I have hated them that holde of supersticiouse vanitees / &
my trust hath bene in the [Lord].
I will be glad and rejoyce in thy mercye / for thu hast consid- 2385
ered my trouble / & hast knowne my sowle in adversitees.
Thu hast not shut me up into the hande of the enemie / but
hast set my fete in a large rowme.

Psalm. xxxi.

Stande up (O lorde God of hostes) thu God of Israel / to 2390
vyset all heathen / and be not mercyfull to them that offende
of malycyouse wickednesse.

Psalm. lix.

G O D   I S.

[Device] 2395

M Y   H E L P E R.

Textual Notes

40		cruelly] cru elly C, T; with bold u B, D, Hn, L, La, Li, M, Ml
41		ressurectyon] [2]r replaced by bold r
56		daungers/] daungersr
60		I am] *C, Hn, Li, T; am I B, D, L, La, M, Ml; Harl 1 and 2
61		deliveraunce] [1]e damaged C, D, Hn, L, Li, T; perfect in B, La, M, Ml
83		infirmytees] ytees—these letters have dropped
102		[1]the] y[e] e clear B, C, L, Ml, T; damaged or blotted in others
117		the] y[t]
155		to delyver] to to delyver
164		fourth] fourh
179		at Melita] *corrected in all copies, except ad Melita B
194		drowned] *corrected in all copies, except drowne B
205		at the last] *at last
207	margin	Bretherne] Bretherue; cropped in La, Ml, T
217		waye·] C, Hn; waye · B, D, L, M, Ml
218		wether dryven] wetherdryven
225		bretherne] brethernc
232		lerne] r damaged Li
246		wonderfull] C, D, Hn, L, M, Ml; r turned and in different type B
249–50		God/which] C, D, Hn, L, M, Ml; God which B
251		me/and] me/ad C, D, Hn, L, M, Ml; me and B

255	Moreover] Morcover
257	salvacion] s faint
268 margin	Prayer] ^{1}r turned
282	DOMINI] *C, Hn, Li, T; DOMIMI B, D, L, La, M, Ml
309	abhominacions] *abohminacions
[310	Bale] Baal (running head)]
318	concernyng] e dropped
329	customehowse] *costomehowse. Ink corr. Hn
330	homely] *homily. Ink corr. Hn
336	synnes] yn dropped
359	Irenaeus] *Irenus. Ink corr. Hn
359	Athanasius] Athanasius'
361	in] iu
406	with] w^t, perhaps w^c (which); with Harl
447	Paule] Panle
448	heavens] hea vens
487	Meduinus] i faint
488	Melanius] *Melaniuus. i doubtful T
512	and] aud B, D, L, Hn, M, Ml; n/u doubtful C, M, T
515	to the] tothe
544	false] falfe
555	transubstanciacion] trasnbstanciacion
566	Barnes/] om. /
574	of] and
576	call] *all. Ink corr. Hn togyther] togither
595	or] *also. als scratched, r added Hn
602	Stoke] *stocke. c scratched Hn
618–20	In . . . counsell] *repeated from fol. 16. Margin subheading changed from The lordes to Lordes
639	gyve] gyne
643	^{1}J.] W. His name was John [Ponet]
668	mainteined by] mainteinedby
674	over] oner, n/u doubtful B, L, Ml
703	olde frynde] oldefrynde
705	superstitions] superstios
712	assistinge] assisinge
719	received] rcceived
770	the bottom righthand corner of fol. 19 is torn off in D, damaging a few letters near the margin. (This has the effect on microfilm STC reel 171 of a "show through" from the lower lefthand corner of fol. 18^v, giving a spurious margin subheading here A trait.)
778	Archebishopp] arhebishopp
782	selfe] felfe
800	men.] men,
804	sowles] solwes

814	doughters] donghters
861	worshyppynges] worsbyppynges : perhaps sh damaged, cf. 1192 shulde/sbulde, 1682 shippe/sbippe
889	Apoca] Apca
929	of so] ofso: ſ damaged C, La; faint Ml, T
944	fledde] fleddde
964	schaddowes] sohaddowes
989	Hothe] *bothe. Ink corr. Hn
990	be] be be
991	was but] *but was
1042	them] chem
1056	with] wᶜ
1071	with an] withan
1086	the] e perhaps damaged
1118	were] where
1123	so] se
1147	clocke] *clocbe. Ink corr. Hn
1151	slewe] flewe
1160	Suffren] Suffreu
[1167	Bale] Bael (running head)]
1171	contray] contrary
1192	shulde] ? sbulde, or h damaged
1210	disdayned] *disdaine
1214	unlearned] vulearned
1228	Antichriste] Autichriste
1230	as I shall] as shall
1264	Rob] Kob
1275	therunto] trerunto
1276	buyldynge] b uyldynge
1284	Irelande] Irelaude, n/u doubtful C
1286	and] aud
1321	againe] aganie
1336	hostes howse] hosteshowse
1341	thought] thonght
1355	an Irishe] *ane Irishe. Ink corr. Hn
1391	myselfe] myselse
1394	and] aud
1405	but] B, C, D, Hn, La, Li, Ml, T; bnt L, M
1410	get] got Harl
1415	sumwhat] s faint B
1417	one] oue
1434	have] hane
1470	apostates] apostataes
1479	Sir James] sir / Iames
1482 margin	fyshes] ? fysbes, or h damaged
1493	unthankefulnesse] unthanke fulnesse

1502	present] r turned
1555	¹the] yᵉ (i.e., the = thee)
1562	²and] of Harl: but "and" can be sustained as "at one with"
1589 margin	Craftie] Crastie
1601	stought] sto ught; gap smaller in B, D, L, M
1602	carryage] carrryage
1607	concluded] coucluded
1646	an] and an Harl
1651	out] ont
1654	of payment] *and payment. Ink corr. Harl
1654	cryed] cred
1660	for] sor
1671 margin	Flaunders] Faunders
1682	shippe] ?sbippe, or h damaged
1684	¹a] om. all but Harl
1688	Fol. 41 lost B
1702	wyth a] wytha
1764	and] aud
1774	Fol. 43 and following pages lost B
1789	present] r turned
1801 margin	nobilite] noiblite
1804	Alphrede] AlPhrede
1820	and] aud C, D, Hn, L, Li, M, Ml, T; u/n doubtful La,
1865	though] thongh
1886	shall] *shalt. Ink corr. Hn
1946	speake] fpeake
1959	farye] ? read fayre
1961	written] writtten
1970 margin	doublenesse] doubleuesse
1973	myght] m turned
1986	for] r turned
1986	suche] suthe
2002	forsaken] sorsaken
2035	No marginal subheadings on this fol. No fol. numbers after fol. 49
2036	patefaction] patefactiou
2073	BAylyfe] BAylfye
2084	Saxons] Saxous
2147	and] aud
2168	murther] mnrther
2169	mansion] mansiou
2170	Horsegrome] ¹r turned
2202	Julius] Julins
2207	favoureth] fanoureth
2214	from] srom

2235	delyveraunce] delyverauuce
2248	mischefe] mischese
2275	Prayer for] Prayerfor; ³r turned
2327	Irelande] Irelan
2358	studye] stndye
2363	pag. 2, li. 14] pag. ii. 14
2368	fol. 13] fo. 13
2371	fol. 16] fo. 16
2372	fol. 24] fo. 24
2377	fol. 40] fo. 40
2378	fol. 45] fo. 45
2384	Lord] om. (*Ego autem in Domino speravi vulg.*)

Running Heads

Fols. 2–8	The preface.
9–17	of Johan Bale. (verso) The Vocacion (recto)
17ᵛ–42ᵛ	The Vocacion (verso) of Johan Bale. (recto) (Vocacion 17; Vocation 1; vocacion 12; vocation 4)
43–49	The conclusion.
G2–G7ᵛ	The table.

Explanatory Notes

6 Ossorye] Diocese in the Province of Dublin, centered on Kilkenny.

39 Math. 3] A meaningless gloss.

51 Hieremye] Jeremiah the prophet.

56 parelouse] *OED* 14th-century form of perilous.

69 byrde which is delivered from the snare of the catcher] Proverbial, see Tilley B 394 ("Birds once snared fear all bushes").

75 Northfolke] Norfolk: Bale was sent to the Carmelite House in Norwich at the age of twelve.

lyddernes] *OED* lidderon, Northern and EA, also PrP. There is no specific link with Norfolk in Tilley's earliest citation for this proverb: C 326 "Better children weep than old men" (Coverdale, 1541).

78 Daniel] Daniel 7:9, 13.

79 devyls vycar at Rome] Term of abuse for the pope. See *Laws* 1585.

80 papistes] Bale employs the terms "papist" and "Christian" in place of "Roman Catholic" and "Protestant." See *OED*.

96 mere] *OED* A2; also in *KJ* 2214.

118 Weston] Hugh Weston (1505?–1558), Rector of Lincoln College, Oxford, 1538–55; Dean of Westminster, 1553–56. Presided over the trial of Thomas Cranmer, Archbishop of Canterbury, and the disputation in Oxford between Hugh Latimer and Richard Smith in 1554. Weston was much vilified by reformers like Bale. See Foxe, *Acts and Monuments*, ed. Cattley, rev. Pratt (1877) 6:439, 501, 503; 8:637; and below, 11.1864–72.

119 breche burninge] ? Sodomy, from ME singular of "breeches."

132 kearnes and galloglasses] Lightly- and heavily-armed infantrymen

maintained by Irish chieftains. See *Macbeth* 1.2.9–13: "The merciless Macdonwald / . . . from the Western Isles / Of kerns and gallowglasses is supplied."

146–48 Damascon . . . Act ix] The ethnarch of King Aretas IV of the Nabateans guarded the gates of Damascus to capture Paul (2 Corinthians 11:32–33, Acts 9:24–25).

151–55 Paules death . . . Actes. 23] Acts 23:23.

156 Barnabe Bolgar] Bale's neighbor and tenant at Holmes Court; see ll. 1061–62.

157 Holmes Court] Bale's residence, five miles from Kilkenny; see l.1057.

166 Zelande] Zeeland, Province of SW Netherlands.

169 Candia] Crete.
  Melita] Malta.

170 Mylforde Haven] A harbor en route between Bristol, where Bale embarked for Ireland, and Waterford (see ll. 658–66).
  Waterforde] The chief Irish port where ships from Bristol, other locations in England, and the Continent disembarked (see l. 665).

172 savegarde] See *Laws*, 1999.

174 Syrtes] Sandbanks off N Africa.

186 vyper] Acts 28:3–6.

196 Publius] Acts 28:7.

200 peltryes] Rubbish, Protestant jargon: see *OED* sb^2 Crowley (1550).

208 Duchelande] Dutchland, or Holland. *OED* 2. See l. 1397.

218 Helias] Elias, i.e., Elijah. See 1 Kings 17:8–24.

226 Germanie / Denmarcke / and Geneva] Havens for English Protestant exiles.

235 receptacles] Places of refuge or retreat, from Lat. *receptaculum*; see *OED* 2.

239 politicall commen welthe] Bale argues against the Erastian belief that the church is completely subordinate to political authority.

247–48 felinge in my self as of my self] "Feeling within myself that my essential nature is . . ."

249 declare] Or "reveal" in the Protestant sense of declaring individual faith; see also *GP*, 27.

282–83 **VERITAS . . . aeternum**] "The truth of the Lord remains forever"; Psalm 116:2 (vulg.). The woodcut portrays Truth carrying a lighted candle symbolic of the light of truth and "VERBUM DEI" (i.e., the Bible). She tramples upon the serpent of error.

285–87 **NOVIT . . . peribit**] "For the Lord knoweth the way of the righteous: but the way of the ungodly shall perish"; Psalm 1:6 (vulg.).

295 adminystracyon] See *OED* administer v. 7, and *Temptation* 352.

301–3 Adam . . . paradyse] Not in Genesis 1–3.

303–4 fathers him succedinng] The patriarchs who lived between the time of Adam and Noah.

314 **Melchisedech**] Ruler of Salem (Jerusalem), considered an ideal priest-king (Genesis 14:17–20, Psalm 110:4).

317 **Zorobabel**] Zoroaster.

321 Aaron] Old Testament type for priesthood or ministry, ancestor of the Hebrew priestly caste.

338 justified] Refers to justification by faith.

344 peculiar] Refers to the Jews as God's chosen people; see *OED* adj. 6.

349 mytered . . . coped . . . typpeted] Protestants attacked the elaborate vestments of the Roman church. The cope is a cloaklike ecclesiastical vestment. The tippet is a long ecclesiastical stole. See also *Laws*, 1181–86.

350 forced] *OED* force v^2; possibly EA (PrP).

pylyoned] †*OED* pillion^2: this is the first citation.

scarletted] A sarcastic reference to the color worn by cardinals. See *KJ*, 1026, et seq.

358 **Tymotheus**] St. Timothy, d. ?97, Bishop of Ephesus, companion and coauthor of St. Paul.

359 **Ignatius**] St. Ignatius, d. ?110, Bishop of Antioch and martyr.

Policarpus] St. Polycarp, d. c. 155–69, bishop and martyr, disciple of St. John who offered hospitality to Ignatius of Antioch during the latter's journey to Rome.

Iren[ae]us] St. Irenaeus, ?140–?202, Bishop of Lyon, disciple of St. Polycarp, opponent of Gnosticism, and Father of the Church. Possibly martyred in Lyon.

Paphnutius] St. Paphnutius, d. ?350, Bishop in the Upper Thebaid, associate of Athanasius and protégé of Constantine.

Athanasius] St. Athanasius, ?297–373, Bishop of Alexandria, persistent opponent of Arianism.

359-60 **Lactantius**] 4th-century apologist and opponent of paganism; his *Divinae institutiones* contrasted pagan and Christian beliefs.

361 vineyearde] John 15:1–5.

361-62 masmongers] Contemptuous term suggesting financial gain. Coined by Bale, first citation, *OED*: *Votaryes* (1550) 2:27

364 Constantine] Emperor Constantine I (?285–337), "the Great," a model for the establishment of secular authority over the church by Henry VIII and his Protestant successors. See l. 1803.

364-65 peace to the Christen churche] After the Battle of Mulvian Bridge (312 A.D.), Emperor Constantine extended toleration and favor to Christianity. The Edict of Milan of the following year granted legal status to the church and brought a formal end to the persecution of Christians.

369 Augustine] St. Augustine, 354–430, Bishop of Hippo, Doctor of the Church, vigorous opponent of Manicheanism. Bale possessed one of his anti-heretical treatises (*Catalogus* 2:166).

388 draught] Matthew 15:17.

398 fatche] Bale's usual spelling, possibly EA, see *GP*, 150.

419 Gildas] First native British historian, ?516–570. He "was born in that time when Roman eloquence flourished most greatly through-

out the entire world," according to Bale, who owned a copy of Gildas' account of the conquest of Britain (*Catalogus* 1:19; 2:159).

423 Japheth] Regarded as the ancestor of the European peoples on the testimony of Genesis 10.

432–34 Luther . . . divided] Martin Luther comments on Genesis 10:5: "Now when the text declares that the islands of the sea were divided by these people [i.e., the sons of Javan], it means that they were skilled in navigating, which they undoubtedly learned from the example of the ark. But since God gave permanence to their rule, I believe that they retained the true forms of worship that they had received from their fathers and that were in use in the church. God overturns the kingdoms of the ungodly and the idolaters; He does not found them." Quoted from *Luther's Works*, 54 vols., ed. Jaroslav Pelikan, et al. (St. Louis, Mo.: Concordia Publishing House, 1955–76) 2:192.

436 Gentilite] The Gentile world; see *OED* II3b.

437 **Berosus**] Priest of Belus in Babylon, 3rd-century B.C. Fragments of his lost history of Babylon are preserved by early Christian writers.
Plinius] Probably Pliny the Younger, b. 61 A.D.
Strabo] Greek historian and geographer, ?64 B.C.-?21 A.D.

438–39 Bale's *Catalogus* 1:93, similarly lists pre-Christian prophets and seers: "Ex illis deinde processerunt Druydes, Bardi, Sibyllae, Vates, Eubages, Flamines, et alij adhuc sub alijs nominibus Gentilium sacerdotes."

438 **Samothees**] Prophets associated with Samothes, the eldest son of the patriarch Japhet (*Catalogus* 1:93).
Sarronites] Prophets associated with Sarron, the successor of Samothes (*Catalogus* 1:93).

439 **Bardes**] Druid priests who recited tribal legends and histories.
Eubages] Priests venerated by the Britons and Gauls.
Vates] Prophets (Lat.)
Flamines] Roman sacrificial priests.

452 Joseph] Joseph of Arimathea, a "secret disciple of Christ" who transmitted Christianity to Britain from the original gospel source according to *Catalogus* 1:15, and Bale's legendary sources. Bale accords Joseph apostolic authority similar to that of St. Paul and St. John the Evangelist in *Summarium*, D1ᵛ-2ᵛ. See *ERL*, 70.

454 **Freculphus**] See his *Chronica* 2.2.4; and *Catalogus* 1:15.

455 **Isidorus**] Isidore of Seville, ?570–636. Bale possessed his *Etymologia* (*Catalogus* 2:165).

459 Italyane writers] ? Polydore Vergil, *Anglicae Historiae Libri XXVI* (Basel, 1534).

460 sanctes legendes] Bale redefined this genre in Protestant terms.

470 Claudia Rufina] 2 Timothy 4:21. This companion of St. Paul was possessed with "humanity, friendship, liberality, piety, learning, study, and Ciceronian eloquence," according to *Catalogus* 1:21.

481 **Bartholomeus Tridentinus**] 13-century Dominican hagiographer,
wrote *Liber Epilogorum* (1245–51).
   Petrus Calo] Pietro Calo, ? 14th-century Dominican monk, author
of lives of St. John of Alexandria, St. Thomas Aquinas, and other
hagiographies.

483–84 Lucius] Legendary king of Britain in succession to his father,
Coilus, according to Geoffrey of Monmouth, *History of the Kings
of Britain* (c. 1136), 4.19. Converted from paganism by a mission from
Pope Eleutherius, he became a patron of the church.

486 mennes tradicions] Bale believed that the early British church continued a direct apostolic tradition going back to Christ, in contrast
to the unwritten "human traditions" that provide the basis of much
Catholic theology.

487–88 **Elvanus . . . Amphibalus**] Learned British churchmen who suc-
ceeded Joseph of Arimathea, according to *Catalogus* 1:22 and 93.

488 **Amphibalus**] Confessor of Albanus, the eponymous saint who was
martyred at St. Albans according to Geoffrey, *History* 5.5.

489 Diocleciane] Valerius Diocletianus, Emperor (284–305), persecu-
tor of Christians.

489–91 Gildas, *De excidio et conquestu Britanniae*, ed. John Josseline
(1568), sect. 7.

492 **Arviragus**] Legendary pagan king of Britain, second son of Cymbe-
line, and great hero during the time of Joseph of Arimathea; see
Geoffrey, *History* 4.12–16; and *Catalogus* 1:15.
   Marius] Legendary pagan king of Britain when Joseph of Arimathea
was buried in Avalon in 76 A.D., son and successor of Arviragus; see
Geoffrey, *History* 4.17, and *Catalogus* 1:16.
   Coillus] Coilus, legendary king of Britain who was loyal to the
church. See *Catalogus* 1:22, and Geoffrey, *History* 4.18.
   Severus] ? Roman general who came to subdue Britain after the death
of Lucius according to Geoffrey, *History* 5.2–3.

496 **Arrius**] Arius, d. 336, condemned as heretic by the Council of Nicaea
in 325, argued that Christ was the most exalted mortal instead of
a divine being; see *Catalogus* 1:35, 37, 93. He and the following heretics "created turmoil in the church because of their allegories" during the peaceful period established by Emperor Constantine
(*Catalogus* 1:93).
   Pelagius] A British or Irish monk who denied original sin and
affirmed free will. The Church of Rome condemned Pelagianism as
a heresy in 416; see *Catalogus* 1:35 and 37.
   Leporius] A follower of Pelagius who was banished from Gaul; see
Catalogus 1:44.
   Tymothe] Proselytized in Britain for the Arian heresy; see *Catalogus* 1:44.

499 monkery] ? A Protestant coinage by Hugh Latimer, cf. *OED* (1536).

500 Antichrist] Identified with the Beast of Revelation 13, this perse-

cutor of the Christian church was identified with the Roman emperor during the first century and with the pope in Rome by Protestants like Bale.

501–5 Bale insists on the independence from Rome of Celtic Christianity in this catalogue of British monks descended from the "pure" apostolic tradition of the early church. According to this view, St. Augustine of Canterbury imported "impure" Roman tradition into Britain.

501 **Fastidius**] "An Evangelist for Christ throughout the whole of Britain" (*Catalogus* 1:40).

502 **Ninianus**] "A man who was assiduously learned in the holy scriptures" (*Catalogus* 1:42).

Patritius] A priest during the pontificate of Celestine I (d. 432), who went to Scotland and Ireland as an anti-Pelagian missionary (*Catalogus* 1:43).

Bachiarius] A "disciple of holy Patritius" (*Catalogus* 1:44).

Dubricius] Opponent of the Arian heresy (*Catalogus* 1:51).

Congellus] An opponent of Pelagianism during the reign of King Arthur (*Catalogus* 1:52–53).

502–3 **Kentigernus**] Opponent of Arianism and Pelagianism c. 560 (*Catalogus* 1:57).

503 **Iltutus**] Said to have preached Christianity openly and to have opposed the "papists" during the reign of King Arthur (*Catalogus* 1:52).

David] A "good" monk said to have studied with Iltutus (*Catalogus* 1:53).

Daniel] Opposed Pelagianism c. 550 (*Catalogus* 1:55–56).

Sampson] Said to have been a good Christian who flourished c. 560 (*Catalogus* 1:57–58).

Elvodugus] Nennius commented on the *History of the British* by this British magistrate according to *Catalogus* 1:60.

504 **Asaphus**] A pious disciple who recorded the life of his master, Kentigernus (*Catalogus* 1:60–61).

Beulanus] A holy priest who followed Elvodugus as the teacher of Nennius (*Catalogus* 1:67).

Elbodus] An opponent of Arianism and Pelagianism who wrote a treatise attacking heresy regarding celebration of the mass (*Catalogus* 1:67).

Dionotus] A monk opposed to the Roman practices brought by Augustine during his mission to England on behalf of Gregory I (*Catalogus* 1:63).

Samuel] The son of Belvanus the priest, and author of a work concerning the reign of King Arthur and annotations on Nennius (*Catalogus* 1:75).

504–5 **Nennius**] Author of the *Historia Britonum* (c. 800), the earliest extant source concerning Arthur and the Matter of Britain.

511 "heathnish Saxons [had subdued] the Christen Britaines. . . ."

516 locustes] Revelation 9:3. Identified by Bale with Roman monks and clergy.

521 **Augustine**] St. Augustine of Canterbury, d. c. 604, first Archbishop of Canterbury, delegated by Pope Gregory I to lead a mission to convert England. In Bale's view, Augustine supplanted the preexisting British church by converting the Saxon invaders; see *ERL*, 70.

522 **Egbert**] St. Egbert of Iona, 639–729, abbot bishop, member of Lindisfarne Abbey and later Iona, where he convinced the community to give up the use of Columba in favor of Roman practice concerning Easter (*Catalogus* 1:91).

Egwine] St. Egwin, d. 717, Bishop of Worcester, founder of Evesham Abbey.

Boniface] St. Boniface, the "apostle of Germany," c. 675–754, monk of Devon, educational reformer, and missionary to Frisia and Germany, Archbishop of Mainz, martyr.

Wilfride] St. Wilfrid, c. 633–709, Archbishop of York.

523 **Dunstane**] St. Dunstan, 924–88, Abbot of Glastonbury and founder of the abbey school, later Archbishop of Canterbury.

Oswolde] Saint Oswald, d. 992, educational reformer, Bishop of Worcester, and later Archbishop of York.

Lanfranck] Lanfranc ?1005–1089, great educator, Archbishop of Canterbury who collaborated with William the Conqueror. Bale possessed a copy of his "dialogus" (*Catalogus* 2:164).

Anselme] St. Anselm, ?1033–1109, theologian and philosopher, abbot of Bec, later Archbishop of Canterbury. Bale possessed his works (*Catalogus* 2:165).

535 **Beda**] The Venerable Bede, 673–735, Benedictine monk at Jarrow, educator and historian, greatest Latin author of the Anglo-Saxon age. His *Historia Ecclesiastica Gentis Anglorum* is the chief authority concerning the conversion of the Angles from paganism. Bale traces his apostolic authority and that of his successors back to Joseph of Arimathea; see comment on l. 452 and *Catalogus* 1:94.

Johan of Beverle] St. John of Beverly, d. 721, Bishop of York, "a man learned in good instruction and pious customs" (*Catalogus* 1:89).

Alcuinus] Alcuin, 735–804, educator and theologian associated with the cathedral school at York.

Neotus] St. Neot, d. c. 900, monk of Glastonbury who became a hermit in Cornwall.

536 **Hucarius**] 11th-century Cornish deacon and theologian who was one of "few in those days, who thrust on behalf of truth, and attacked the innumerable superstitions that had crawled into the church" (*Catalogus* 1:152).

Serlo] Monk of Dover or Canterbury (*Catalogus* 1:136).

Achardus] Canon of the monastery at Bridlington in Yorkshire, known for his philosophical and theological learning (*Catalogus* 1:182).

Ealredus] d. 1166, abbot and scholar at the Cistercian monastery at Rievaulx in Yorkshire (*Catalogus* 1:208-9).

Alexander Neckam] 1157-1217, Augustinian Abbot of Cirencester, wrote *De Naturis Rerum*.

537 **Nigellus]** Nigel Wireker, flourished c. 1180, monk and satirist, author of *Speculum Stultorum* (*The Mirror for Fools*), which attacks ecclesiastic and social corruption (*Catalogus* 1:245-46). Bale possessed this satire (*Catalogus* 2:163).

Sevallus] d. 1258, Archbishop of York who was "continually opposed to Antichrist" (*Catalogus* 1:311-12).

539 **schole doctours]** The "Schoolmen" or Scholastic philosophers of the High Middle Ages.

539-40 **four ordres]** Franciscan, Dominican, Carmelite, and Austin friars.

541 **sophisticall]** See *OED*, "sophistycall sorceryes," *Votaries* 2:116b, *KJ*, 3.

543 **sinagoge of Sathan]** Protestant jargon for the Catholic church, alludes to Revelation 2:9; see *OED* 2.

550-51 **registre . . . Englande]** ? Register of the monastic visitations at the time of the Dissolution of the Abbeys. The full extent of Bale's library is not now known, but see Honor McCusker, "Books and Manuscripts Formerly in the Possession of John Bale," *The Library*, 4th ser., 16 (1936): 144-65.

558 **gaddinge]** *OED* vbl. sb.^{2}, *Apology* (1550) 108b.

559 **gossippes]** Usually godparents *OED* 1.a; also "female friends."

561-62 **palpable darkenesse]** Exodus 10:21, *Laws* 1803.

563 **Mathew Parys]** Matthew (of) Paris, monk of St. Albans, c. 1190-1259, whose *Greater Chronicle* documents English history from the Norman Conquest to 1259.

Oclyf] Thomas Hoccleve, c. 1368-?1450, clerk of the Privy Seal Office, known chiefly for his 1411 *De regimine principum* (*The Regiment of Princes*).

563-64 **Wickleff]** John Wyclif, c. 1328-1384, ecclesiastical reformer, sponsor of the first complete translation of the Bible into English. Bale viewed himself as Wyclif's successor in an apostolic succession going back to Joseph of Arimathea, and he owned his works. See *Catalogus* 1:450; 2:163. See also *ERL*, 70.

564 **Thorpe]** William, d. 1407, disciple of Wyclif; subject of *The examinacion of Master William Thorpe preste*, possibly edited by William Tyndale (Antwerp, 1530; *STC* 24045). Bale owned a copy of his interrogation for heresy ("examinatio per episcopos"; *Catalogus* 2:166). See also *Catalogus* 1:538.

White] William, d. 1428, a disciple of Wyclif, burnt as a heretic (*Catalogus* 1:564-65).

Purveye] John Purvey, ?1353-?1428, disciple of Wyclif who rendered the Bible translation associated with his mentor into a more freely readable vernacular version. Likely author of a biblical prologue edited and published in 1550 by Bale's associate, Robert Crowley (*STC* 25588); see *ERL*, 97–99.

Pateshulle] Peter Pateshull, author of a Wyclifite commentary on Hildegard's prophecy against the friars that Bale lists among the publications of Robert Crowley (c. 1550); see *Catalogus* 1:509–10, and *ERL*, 477. Bale owned a copy of Pateshull's *"de Vitis fratrum Mendicantium: uel eius commentarius in prophetiam Hyldegardis, cum rhythmis facetissimis"* (*Catalogus* 2:160).

Paine] Peter Paine, flourished 1436, "he was a most constant disciple and follower of John Wyclif and his disciples in the sincere doctrine of truth" (*Catalogus* 1:578).

564–65 Gower] John Gower, c. 1330–1408, author of *Confessio Amantis*. Bale possessed his *Chronica tripartita* (*Catalogus* 2:160).

565 Chaucer] Praised by Bale as a crypto-Protestant reformer (*Catalogus* 1:525–27).

Gascoigne] Thomas Gascoigne, 1403–58, Oxford theologian and Chancellor of the university, opponent of ecclesiastical abuses and the holding of multiple benefices. Bale possessed his theological dictionary (*Catalogus* 2:163).

Ive] William Ive or Ivy, d. 1485, Oxford theologian, later Chancellor of the diocese of Salisbury.

565–66 William Tindale] Tyndale, c. 1494–1536. Bale regards this reformer as Wyclif's direct apostolic successor (*Summarium*, 314ᵛ).

566 Johan Frith] John Frith, 1503–33, Protestant reformer who assisted Tyndale in translating the New Testament, executed at Smithfield as a heretic.

Bilneye] Thomas Bilney, c. 1495–1531, first-generation Protestant, iconoclastic preacher, executed as a heretic.

Barnes] Robert Barnes, 1495–1540, first-generation Protestant, burnt as a heretic.

Lambert] John (his real surname was Nicholson), d. 1538, first-generation English Protestant, burnt as a heretic.

567–77 lattre age . . . of thys age] Bale regards the religious reformation led by the Protestant clergy as a sign of the imminence of the Last Judgment. See also his *Image of Both Churches*.

572–73 destruction of Hierusalem] By Roman legions following the rebellion of the Jews, 70 A.D.

580 Golias of Rome] The Roman Goliath, i.e., the pope.

583 David] Regarded by Bale and other Protestants as a type for Henry VIII as a pious yet flawed monarch who initiated an incomplete process of religious reformation.

thys buyldynge] The Temple in Jerusalem was a type for the "true" Christian church.

584 Salomon] Solomon, type for Edward VI as a reformist monarch who completed reforms that his father left undone.

586 Hieroboam] Jeroboam I, an apostate king (1 Kings 12:1–14:20). Bale

views his reign as a prototype for Mary Tudor's restoration of Roman Catholic practices.

587 Samaria] The region of Israel where Jeroboam established his capital, Shechem. Bale confuses this area with the neighboring district of Bethel, where the king set up one of two golden calves as idols (1 Kings 12:28–30).

590 Asa] This king destroyed idols and forbade worship at pagan shrines (1 Kings 15:9–24).

Josaphat] Jehosophat, King of Judah, 2 Chronicles 19:4–11.

591 Ezechias] Hezekiah, King of Judah, 2 Chronicles 31:2. According to KJ, 1512–13, Jehosophat and Hezekiah had power to appoint the Hebrew priests because they were rulers anointed by God.

Josias] He implemented Deuteronomic reform by destroying pagan idols, images, and shrines in the Kingdom of Judah (2 Kings 22:1–23:30). Regarded by Bale, Crowley, and other reformers as a type for Edward VI as an iconoclastic monarch who instituted legitimate reforms in the church despite his status as a minor (ERL, 161, 177, 185–86).

602 Bysshoppes Stoke] Bishopstoke ("the holy place of the bishop," from OE "biscop" +"stoc"), a town in Hampshire six miles south of Winchester. As Rector of the Church of St. Mary and chaplain to John Ponet, who occupied the adjacent manor of the Bishop of Winchester, Bale lived "within the bishopes howse there" (ll. 651–52; see also ERL, 112–13). He describes his 1551–52 efforts to convert the local populace in An Expostulation or Complaynte agaynste the Blasphemyes of a Franticke Papyst of Hamshyre (c. 1552).

607 Johan Fylpot] John Philpot (1516–55), Edwardian courtier, executed as a heretic under Mary I. Bale attributes his appointment to the bishopric of Ossory to Philpot's good offices.

626 B. Hamptone] Bernard Hampton, Clerk of the Privy Council, 24 September 1551–6 July 1553.

643 [J.] Winchestre] John Ponet, Bishop of Winchester, 23 March 1551-August 1553. During their exile under Mary I, Ponet deferred to Bale as his senior and literary mentor (ERL, 113).

J. Bedford] John Russell, c. 1485–1555, first Earl of Bedford, Keeper of the Privy Seal.

H. Suffolke] Henry Grey, 1517–54, father of Lady Jane Grey, created Duke of Suffolk on 11 October 1551, forfeited title on 17 February 1554, executed on 23 February 1554.

644 W. Northampton] William Parr, 1513–71, Marquis of Northampton, forfeited title August 1553.

T. Darcy] Sir Thomas Darcy, fl. 1550–53, first Baron Darcy of Chiche, Chamberlain of the Household (1551–53), supporter of Northumberland.

T. Cheine] Sir Thomas Cheyne, ?1485–1558, Treasurer of Household and Warden of the Cinque ports.

Johan Gate] Sir John Gates ?1504–1553, privy councillor, Vice Chamberlain, and Chancellor of the Duchy of Lancaster.

W. Cecill] William Cecil, 1520–98, Principal Secretary of State, 1550–53.

651 age] At fixty-six, Bale was quite old by sixteenth-century standards.

659 bokes] Bale brought a large library with him to Ireland (*Catalogus* 2:159–67). See McCusker's annotated edition of Bale's own shelf list in "Books and Manuscripts," 149–62; and ll. 550, 1365, 1509.

659–60 Bristowe] Bristol; see note on l. 170.

671–72 bowynges and beckynges / knelinges] Ritual gestures accompanying the celebration of the Roman-rite mass. The "Black Rubric" added to the second *Book of Common Prayer* (1552) explained that this act of veneration implied no belief in transubstantiation. See *Laws*, 1430 concerning "beckynges."

672 knockinges] Penitential beating of the breast in ritual.

674–76 prodigyouse howlynges and patterynges . . . passion] Bale objects to Roman ritualism and to keening (loud wailing for the dead) that survived from pagan times.

677–78 Requiem Eternam] Opening words of introit of the mass for the dead, "Requiem aeternam dona eis, Domine." Protestants rejected masses for the dead on the ground that Christ is the all-sufficient savior and source of redemption (ll. 805, 1006–8).

680 Senatour] Member of the town's governing body.

685 Knocktover] Knocktopher, town twelve miles S of Kilkenny, en route to Waterford.

687 Syr Philypp] ? Variant of "Sir John," a satirical appelation for a priest (*OED* John 3). "Sir" could be placed before the Christian name of priests as a translation of Lat. *dominus* (*OED* Sir 4).

702 Hugh Goodaker] Hugh Goodacre, consecrated Archbishop of Armagh on 2 February 1553, died 1 May 1553. Recruited by the English government along with Bale, who had known him at Bishop Ponet's house in Winchester (*Catalogus* 2:109, 231), to implement radical religious reform in Ireland (Bradshaw, 93–94).

Armach] Armagh, one the four provinces of the Church of Ireland, the others being Cashel, Dublin, and Tuam.

703 David Coper] Or Cooper (?), parson of Callan, County Kilkenny, nine miles SW of Kilkenny.

707 purificacion daye] February 2, festival of the presentation of Christ in the Temple by the Virgin Mary upon the completion of her purification (Luke 2:22).

708 Thomas Cusake] Cusack, Chief Governor and Lord Justice of Ireland (with Sir Gerald Aylmer), 9 December 1552–19 November 1553. A protégé of Anthony St. Leger (see note on l. 1324).

710 George] Browne, Archbishop of Dublin, 1536–54, chief supporter of Protestant reform in Ireland (Bradshaw, 83, 91), deprived 1554, d. 1556. He urged the appointment of zealots like Bale to head the dio-

ceses in his province: Ossory, Leighlin, and Kildare (Edwards, 127).
Bale's vilification of him as a crypto-papist was presumably moti-
vated both by the prelate's ignorance of the second *Book of Com-
mon Prayer* (see note on l. 724) and by his desire to obtain half of
Bale's living for the first year of his bishopric; see the attack on "olde
George" at ll. 1298–1336.

711 Thomas] Lancaster, deprived of his bishopric in 1554.

712 Urbane] Although this name has not been traced, there is another
reference at *Catalogus* 2:109. The second officiating bishop was Eu-
gene Magennis of Down (Bagwell, 379).

719 imposicion of handes] The forms for ordaining ministers and consecrating bishops in the first and second versions of the Edwardian
Book of Common Prayer retained the traditional laying on of hands
(see Acts 13:3, 1 Timothy 4:14).

720 Thomas Lockwode] Dean of Christ Church, Dublin, 1543–1565.

724 boke of consecratinge] "The Forme of Consecrating of an Arche-
bisshoppe or Bysshoppe" in the second *Book of Common Prayer* of
Edward VI (1552) replaced the traditional form found in the first Edwardian prayer book. Archbishop Browne's ignorance of this ordinal
scandalized Bale, who demanded its use at his consecration. See note
on l. 847.

767 traded with] †*OED*, v. 5 (1562): this is the first citation.

770 Aethna] Mount Etna or Aetna.

801 whyte Goddes] Mass wafers, assumed to be transubstantiated into
the body of Christ. See ll. 1108–10.

809–10 chauntynge / pypynge / and syngynge] Bale and other Protestants were critical of liturgical music; see *Select Works of John Bale*,
ed. Henry Christmas, Parker Soc., vol 36 (Cambridge, 1849), 536.

847 boke of commen prayer] *The Boke of Common Prayer and Administracion of the Sacramentes, and Other Rites and Ceremonies in the
Churche of England*, 2nd version (1552). Bale was on doubtful ground
here because only the 1549 prayer book had been legally proclaimed
in Ireland. The English privy council approved of an Irish translation of the prayer book (Bradshaw, 90).

865 assension daye] 11 May 1553.

868 poysened] See Bradshaw, 94.

879 Rob davie] "Metheglin," spiced mead.
    aqua vite] Whiskey, from Med. Lat. "aqua vitae" ("water of life").
See l. 1136.

881 Gaudeamus in dolio] Irish priests welcomed King Edward's death
by drinking in taverns and singing this parodic song ("Let us rejoice
in sorrow").

883 Kynge Edwarde was dead] It took nearly three weeks before this
news of Edward's death reached Kilkenny.

884 maskynge] Refers to the masque, a form of entertainment still associated with Italy according to Hall's *Chronicle* (1548), Henry VIII,

16: "The kyng with eleven other were disguised, after the maner of Italie, called a maske, a thyng not seen afore in Englande." Frequently used in derogatory references to the Mass. See *OED* masque 1; masking vbl. sb.[2], 1b.

892 Thomas Hothe] ? Thomas Houth (or Howth), Chief Remembrancer of the Exchequer in 1541, Justice and Royal Commissioner in 1549.

894 Communion . . . S. Anne] In forbidding a communion service on St. Anne's day (26 July), Bale decries the "blasphemouse" observation of saints' festivals on weekdays.

919 Ladye Jane Gylforde] Née Grey, the "nine-day queen" who was proclaimed queen in Kilkenny on 27 July, a full week after her deposition in London.

928 deputye] The Lord Deputy, Sir James Croft (or Crofts), appointed in 1551, and recalled in 1552. His militance accorded with the zealous progress of religious reform under John Dudley, Earl of Warwick, after the fall of Edward Seymour, Duke of Somerset and Protector of the Realm of England.

934 Earle of Ormonde] Thomas Butler, 1531–1614, Earl of Ossory and Ormond. A member of the old Anglo-Norman community.

935 Barne] Baron.

943 Mathew Kinge] Clerk of the Check (Bagwell, 383).

948 Mihell Patricke] "Barne" or Baron of Upper Ossory.
Mountgarret] Uncle of the Earl of Ormonde.

953 proclamed Quene] Slowness in communications necessitated the thirty-three day delay in the proclamation of Mary I's accession.

961 Moyses minister] Minister of Moses, i.e., Roman priest?

970–72 disgysed . . . pageauntes] Bale attempted to supplant this spectacle with performances of his own polemical dramas. He and other Protestants attacked Catholic processions in honor of Corpus Christi and other feast days, and the dramatic tableaux and performances that accompanied them, as non-scriptural practices. See ll. 1100–2, 1263.

972 pageauntes] tricks *OED* sb. 1c, following Wyclif.

973 *A Tragedye or Enterlude manyfestyng the Chefe Promyses of God, A Brefe Comedy or Enterlude of Johan Baptystes Preachyng in the Wyldernesse*, and *A Brefe Comedy or Enterlude Concernynge the Temptacyon of our Lorde* had been compiled by Bale c. 1538 and printed probably by Dirik van der Straten at Wesel, in the County of Cleves, in 1547.

974–75 organe plainges and songes] Bale arranged singing and musical accompaniment by a portatif or portable organ for an open-air production of his dramatic trilogy.

979–80 S. Bartylmewes daye] August 24.

984–85 **non** . . . **credenti**] "For I am not ashamed of the gospel: it is the power of God for salvation to everyone who has faith"; Romans 1:16 (vulg.).

1004 derogacion . . . honour] See Moses' attack against "Worshyppynge false goddes to thy [God's] honours derogacyon" in Bale's *GP*, 514.

1012-13 **Beati oculi qui vident. . . .**] "Blessed are the eyes which see what you see" (Luke 10:23).

1019-28 wounded man . . . charges] Parable of the Good Samaritan (Luke 10:29-37).

1020 levite] Assistant to the Hebrew Temple priests.

1021-22 Samaritaine] Bale's reference to contemptuousness (i.e., superiority) diverges from the gospel account of the Samaritan who showed compassion to the wounded man.

1034-35 purgatorye . . . dead] Prohibited Catholic practices.

1035 suffrages] *OED* sb. 1b; *KJ* 1045, PrP.

1053 devill in the wildernesse] Luke 4:1-13. Bale dramatizes this event in *Temptation*, 209-42, referring to Psalm 90:11-12 (vulg.).

1059 Routhe] ? Sir Richard Howth, Treasurer of St. Canice's (see Bagwell, 388).

1071 brechelesse] *KJ*, 710.

1087-94 The local clergy restored Catholic sacramental practices without official sanction or Bale's consent.

1098-99 candelstickes . . . crosse] Edward VI's *Injunctions* (1547) forbade "woorkes devised by mannes phantasies, besides [in place of] scripture: as . . . offeryng of money, candelles or tapers, to Reliques, or Images, or kissing and lickyng of the same" (item 2). They ordered clergy to destroy devotional images and to "suffre from hencefurthe, no Torches, nor candelles, Tapers or Images of waxe, to be sette afore any Image or picture, but onelye twoo lightes upon the high aulter, . . . whiche, for the significacion, that Christe is the very true light of the worlde, thet shall suffre to remain styll" (item 3). In 1551 Archbishop Browne accused Archbishop Dowdall of Armagh of refusing to prohibit " 'holy water, Christmas candles and such like' " (Bradshaw, 85). See *Injunctions*, item 11.

1099 sensers] Censers.

1100-1102 procession . . . latine Letanie] Edward VI's *Injunctions* stipulate that no one should "use any procession, about the Churche or Churche yarde, or other place, but immediatly before highe Masse, the priestes with other of the queire, shal kneele in the middes of the churche, and synge or saye, plainly and distinctely, the Letany, which is setfurthe in English, with all the Suffrages folowyng, and none other Procession, or Letany to be had or used, but the sayed Letanie in Englishe. . . . and all ringynge and knowlynge [i.e., tolling] of Belles, shalbe utterly forborne for that tyme, excepte one Belle, in conveniente tyme, to be rong or knowled before the Sermon" (item 23). See *OED* litany 1.

1101 Sancta Maria ora pro nobis] "Holy Mary, pray for us."

1104-5 from the grace of God into a warme sunne] to go from a better to a worse situation. †*OED* God, sb. 5c (1562). ? Ironic here.

1122 eare confession] Auricular confession, for which the *Book of Common Prayer* substituted a general confession of faith on the part of the entire congregation. Bale sees it as an instrument of sedition in *KJ*, 267–73.

1125 bishop of Galwaye] No diocese of Galway existed during the sixteenth century. Although Bale may refer to John Mor, Bishop of Enachdun (Annadown), he probably refers to the Archbishop of Tuam, whose province contained Galway and the diocese of Enachdun (Edwards, 160).

1131–35 Confirmacion] The order for "Confirmacion, Wherin is Conteined a Catechisme for Children" stipulates that every curate "openly in the churche instructe and examine so many children of his parish sent unto him, as the time wil serve, and as he shal thynke conveniente, in some parte of this Catechisme. . . . And whansoever the Bushop shal geve knowledge for children to be brought afore [i.e., before] him to any convenient place, for their confirmacion: Then shal the curate of every parish either bring or send in writing, the names of al those children of his parish which can say tharticles of theyr faith, the lordes praier, and the ten commandementes. And also how many of them can answere to thother questions conteined in this Catechisme" (*BCP 1*).

1132–33 over the English part] ? Within the Pale, the Anglicized region surrounding Dublin, included in the royal dominions.

1142–52 Another violent encounter between one of Bale's retainers and a local inhabitant is recorded in the "Corporation Book of the Irishtown of Kilkenny," fol. 4, which states: "it happened that there was weapons drawn by one named Call, servante to John Bale, Bishopp of Ossery, within the Lord Bishopp [h]is house, againste Laurence Power, of the Irishtown, burgess." The Portrive of Kilkenny meted out a penalty for "the frayes and bloodsheds don in the sayd Lord Bishopp manor house." Transcribed in *Analectica Hibernica*, no. 28 (1978), 8.

1156–57 maistre Coopers] ? See l. 703.

1173–74 holye daye . . . nativite] 8 September.

1216–18 tempte . . . stones] Matthew 4:3–4, Luke 4:1–13. See Bale's *Temptation*, 104–12; and ll. 1053–55.

1224 Requiem . . . Dirige] Masses and matins for the dead had been prohibited under Edward VI. The antiphon at matins in the Latin office of the dead begins: "Dirige, Domine, Deus meus, in conspectu tuo viam meam."

1238–43 preste disgysed . . . good wurde] Bale attacks the mass as a dramatic spectacle in which the priest elevates the host in front of the congregation before turning toward the altar to continue reciting in Latin. He may refer to impromptu performances that precede requests for money and applause by jugglers or magicians. See note on ll. 970–72; and *ERL*, 135–36.

1243 Orate . . . fratres] "Pray for me, brothers." An extra-liturgical prayer formula.
1244–45 Dominus vobiscum] "Lord be with you." Part of the order of
the mass.
1246–47 Benedictio Dei] "Blessing of God." An extra-liturgical prayer
formula.
1262 Thomas towne] Thomastown, ten miles SE of Kilkenny.
1276 that buyldynge] See note on l. 583.
1291 colligyners] See *OED*, collegianer, *Votaryes* 3.
1296 Lechline] Leighlin, a diocese in the Province of Dublin.
1298–1300 Epicurouse archebishop . . . hande] See note on l. 710. The
Injunctions of Edward VI stipulate that "after their Dynner and
Supper" clerics "shall not geve themselfes to drinckyng or riot" (item
8).
1303–4 preciouse pearles . . . swine] Matthew 7:6.
brockish] *Votaryes* 1:8b, *OED*.
1308 Sardinapalus] Sardanapalus, last king of Assyria, an effete prince
who was overthrown in 880 B.C.
1308–13 preachinges] Browne allegedly violates the authorized practice
of the Church of England by memorizing two sermons that varied
only with the seasons. Item 32 of Edward VI's *Injunctions* stipulates
that "all Persones [i.e., parsons], Vicars, and Curates, shall reade in
their Churches, every Sondaye, one of the Homelies, whiche are and
shalbe setfurthe, for thesame purpose, by the Kynges aucthoritie"
(i.e., the *Book of Homilies*).
1309–10 Exit qui seminat] "A man went out to sow" (Luke 8:5; vulg.).
1310–11 Ego . . . bonus] "I am the good shepherd" (John 10:14; vulg.).
1316–17 Debethes] ? A practitioner treating venereal diseases.
1318 hobby] Pony, usually Irish (*OED*), but here perhaps "whore."
1324 Antony Sellenger] Sir Anthony St. Leger, Lord Deputy in 1540–48,
1550–51, 1553. A believer in conciliation and moderate Protestant
reform who supported appointment of local clergy instead of evangelical immigrants like Bale. Archbishop Browne opposed his flexi-
ble policy of long-range ecclesiastical modification and contributed
to his replacement by Croft (Bradshaw, 91–92; see note on l. 928).
1336 Estsexe] The County of Essex.
1373–74 maistre Parker / the searcher] ? A customs official.
1400–1 Nortwyck] Northwych (Noordwijk), village near Leiden, Holland, where Sartorius (1500–67), humanist and friend of Bale,
preached.
1443 dronke as an ape] Proverbial; see Tilley, A265, Whiting A140.
bone viage] Bon voyage, or safe journey.
1456 temple] Church.
1460 lubber] Lout, frequently applied to monks, *OED* sb. 1; see *KJ*, 36.
1468 Myles Coverdale] Miles Coverdale, c. 1488–1569, a successor of
Tyndale. St. Ives belonged in his diocese as Bishop of Exeter (1551–53).

Bale later described him as "a poor man and an exile in Germany" (*Catalogus* 1:721).

1481–82 howsellar] Houseler, priest who administers the Eucharist, used in a sarcastic sense; see *OED* housel, 1.

1483–84 my maker] i.e., the consecrated host. The sacrilegious priest used the element of bread from the service of holy communion as fish bait.

1493 plage] Exodus 7–10.

1493–94 unthankefulnesse whyls we had the truthe] Refers to the period of Edward VI's Protestant ascendancy. See l. 1786 and note.

1538 Britaine] Brittany.

1544 Lynne] King's Lynn, a major port in Norfolk.

1555 laye the fast] †*OED* lay, 25b (1560).

1564–65 Doctour Gardiner] Stephen Gardiner, newly restored Bishop of Winchester and Lord Chancellor of Queen Mary, vilified for persecuting Protestants; see *Catalogus* 1:685–86.

1571 **Gesnerus**] Konrad von Gesner, 1516–65, German-Swiss Protestant naturalist and author. Bale dedicated the thirteenth "century" (100 author entries) of his *Catalogus* to Gesner, whose own universal bibliography, *Bibliotheca universalis* (Zurich, 1545), is similar in kind to Bale's compendia.

1572 **Alesius**] Of Scottish origin, supported by Cromwell against John Stokesley, Bishop of London (*Catalogus* 2:227–28).

   Pellicanus] Konrad Pellicanus, 1478–1556, Hebrew scholar, priest, Protestant convert, and professor in Protestant Zurich.

   Pomeranus] Johann Bugenhagen, 1485–1558, coadjutor of Luther in N. Germany.

1573 **Melancthon**] Philipp Melanchthon, 1497–1560, German Protestant reformer, disciple of Luther.

   Camerarius] 1500–74, classical scholar and disciple of Melanchthon.

1574 **Flacius**] Matthias Flacius Illyricus (Mattias Vlachich), 1520–75, Croatian Lutheran whose career as a strident polemicist paralleled that of Bale. Concerning his interest in Bale's library, see Introduction, "Life and Works."

1575 Antiquytees and doctrines] As the successor of John Leland, Bale attempted to enumerate and preserve manuscripts and printed books that were in danger of destruction because of the Henrician dissolution of monastic houses (*ERL*, 67, 98). Bale edited and expanded Leland's *Laboryouse Journey and Serche for Englandes Antiquitees* (1549).

1642–43 at a point] See *OED* sb^1, point, D.1.d; *KJ*, 1489.

1644 hag / tag / rag] Rabble, riffraff; also called "ragtag and bobtail." Tilley T10, first instance.

1646 Cerberus] Three-headed dog that guarded the entrance to the underworld.

1698–99 Andwerpe] Antwerp.

1709 embassadours at Brucels] Marian ambassadors to the Spanish Netherlands.

1712 Lovayne] Louvain, city in Spanish Netherlands.

1713 Rabyes] Rabbis, learned men (contemptuous *OED* 2b).

1754–56 belles . . . lyghtes] Edward VI's *Injunctions* prohibited the superstitious use of "Images, and other deede [i.e., dead] thynges . . . or ringynge of the holy Belles, or blessyng with the holy candell, to thintent, therby to be discharged of the burden of synne, or to dryve awaye devilles, or to put away dreames and Phantasies, or in puttynge truste and confidence of healthe and salvacion, in thesame Ceremonies" (item 27). See ll. 1098–99.

1759 fanne] Matthew 3:12, Luke 3:17. This image of God's judgment as a threat to "hypocrytes" appears in *JBP*, 328–33.

harvest] A notable apocalyptic trope (Matthew 13:39, Revelation 14:15).

1768 plage] See note on l. 1493.

1786 visitacion] *OED* II.6a; here possibly referring to the reign of Edward VI.

1796 Pygion of Paules] Prostitute practicing in the vicinity of St. Paul's Cathedral; analogous to the appellation "goose of Winchester" for women in brothels that were located in Southwark within the jurisdiction of the Bishop of Winchester (see *Troilus and Cressida* 5.10.54). †*OED* pigeon 3 (1568).

1803 **Nycodeme**] Nicodemus, a Pharisee who became a secret follower of Christ.

Kynge Lucius] See ll. 483–84.

Justinyane] Justinian I, 483–565, "the Great," Byzantine emperor and promulgator of the Justinian Code.

1804 **Theodosius**] Theodosius I, ?346–395, "the Great," emperor of the Eastern Roman Empire who made Christianity the official state religion of the Roman empire.

Alphrede] Alfred the Great, 849–899, King of the West Saxons. See *Catalogus* 1:125–26.

Ethelstane] Aethelstan, King of Wessex (acceded 925), whose 927 annexation of the Kingdom of York led to the submission of the other kings of Britain. He was the first Saxon to become paramount ruler of the island.

1820 Antiochus] Antiochus IV Epiphanes, Seleucid king of Syria, provoked the revolt of the Maccabees by trying to convert the Jews.

1823–24 **Foelix . . . cautum**] Not in concordance.

1833–34 **Mycheas . . . Sedechias**] 2 Chronicles 18:23–24.

1834 **Parali**] Paralipomenon (Chronicles in the Vulgate Bible).

Helias] See note on l. 218.

1836 **Esaye**] Isaiah.

1838 **Hieremie**] Jeremiah.

Semeias] Jeremiah 29:29–32.

1845 **Antipas**] Revelation 2:13.

1846 Simon Magus] Acts 8:9–24.

1847 **Johan Zebede**] John the Apostle, son of Zebedee (Matt. 4:21); reputed to have prophesied on Patmos (Rev. 1:9).

1847–48 **Cerinthus, Menander**] Early Gnostic thinkers.

1848 **Hebion**] Ebion, the supposed founder of the Ebionite movement, an early Christian sect influenced by Judaism.

1866 St Botolphes parishe] See John Stow, *The Survey of London*, ed. H. B. Wheatley, rev. ed. (London, 1965), 148.

1871–72 **Mulier . . . est**] Bale appears to be quoting the following Vulgate text from memory: "Mulier alligata est legi quanto tempore vir ejus vivit, quod si dormierit vir ejus, liberata est" (1 Cor. 7:39). Weston allegedly misused the scripture by taking the literal sense of the verb "to sleep" instead of the metaphorical "to die."

1874 priapustick] Not cited in †*OED*, but see Priapus 4.

1885–88 Practices forbidden by the royal *Injunctions* (item 27).

1888 laye mennis Gospell] Protestants rejected the Gregorian directive that "images are the laymen's books." Although Pope Gregory I did not intend that devotional images supplant the Bible in lay religious instruction, he did allow that "in the same thing [i.e., the picture] they read [the truth] who do not understand letters. Whence and especially to the [common] people the picture is in place of reading" (*Patrologiae cursus completus. Series latina*, ed. J.-P. Migne, 221 vols. [Paris, 1844–64] 77: col. 1128.

1889 Porphirius] Porphyry of Tyre, 233–304, a Neoplatonist, wrote a treatise in fifteen books against the Christians that survives only in fragmentary form. Eusebius of Caesarea (c. 260–c. 340) replied to it in *Praeparatio Evangelica*.

1891–92 S. Gregorie the great] Gregory I, ?540–604, pope; Bale possessed his works (*Catalogus* 2:165).

1895 **Epiphanius**] St. Epiphanius of Constantia, bishop and Father of the Church, ?315–402, noted for writings against heresies, and for devotion to the Virgin.

1899–1900 Sancte . . . nobis] A non-liturgical invocation to St. Peter.

1909 Coyne and lyverie] Irish custom of billeting men and horses upon private persons, *OED* coynye (from Irish).

1937 the Englishe pale] See note on ll. 1132–33.

1973 effectually] †*OED* 3 (1583).

1978–79 churche of Englande] Bale defines his audience as the congregation of English Protestants, whose backsliding is the alleged cause of persecution and suffering under Mary I. In the *Image of Both Churches* and other works, he characteristically presents the "true" church as the opposite of "Malignaunt churche of the papistes" (ll. 1993–94).

1989 frowardnesse] See frowarde *GP*, 686; *KJ*, 1657.

2060 The table] The numbers in the table refer to the folio numbers, both recto and verso.

2379–80 Rome . . . S. Peter] This conventional satirical colophon presents Bale figuratively as one who preaches against error at the seat of papal power.

2395 Hugh Singleton's device incorporates his mark, his initials, and a rebus portraying a single tun.

Appendix

James Cancellar included the following attack on Bale's *Vocacyon* in *The pathe of Obedience, righte necessarye for all the king and Quenes majesties loving Subjectes* (*STC* 4564, London, ?1556), sigs. D3ʳ-7ʳ. He wrote this orthodox appeal for obedience to royal authority as a chaplain to Mary I, to whom he dedicated the text. See Introduction, "Reception."

. . . I am sure saith saint Paule, of this, that after my departinge shall grevous wolves enter in among you, not sparinge the flocke, and also of youre owne selves shall menne aryse, speaking perverse thinges to draw disciples after them. Have not good contremen the like Wolves entred among us in this realme? Grafting in the vyneyard of our lord, thornes and brambles, and also drawing christes members from the true obedience and discipline of their mother the catholike church. As of late manye hath rysen amonge us in this realme, and especially that presumpteous heretike John Bale, who hath taken no smale travaile to hinder through his abhominable heresies, the glory of Christes gospel. As it doth appeare by divers and sundry bokes by him made, and speciallye in his boke intiteled the vocacion of John Balle to the bishoprike of Ossery where he not a litle triumpheth of hys daungerous travailes whyche he had in the same, not shaming to compare himselfe with holy saincte Paul in troubles, in labours, in perill of shipe wracke, in perill of the sea, in perill of false brethren, in peril of pirates, robbers and murtherers. This whilest he is comparing himself with the holy Apostle lyke a mad harehead begynneth to say why shoulde I shrinke or bee a shamed to boste as the Apostle hath? Who as it appereth in the seconde to the Corinthians (saith he) dyd boste of hys labours perils and troubles in the gospell. And the lyke laboure and perilles had I in my Jorneye with no lesse trouble then he had from Jerusalem to Rome, saving that sayeth he we loste not our ship, and in the seventh lefe and on the lefte syde he sayeth, I wryhte not this for that I would receive prayse hereof, But that I have done it also to declare my most earnest reioice in the same god, which by grace hath called me, by persecucyon hath tried me, and of favoure hath most wonderfully delivered me. Here Frier Bale beginneth craftely to perswade with the poore Christians that GOD hath delivered him from peril of death by miracle as thoughe he were called of god in these daies to set up a light in his churche: but as that notable heretyke cerinthus did labour to put oute of the Churche of God the true lyght of the gospell in the time of the holy apostle Saint John so doth that shameles freer laboure and travaile all that he may, lyke a false disciple, to put forth himselfe and to tread downe in these our dayes the true light of the gospell wherefore freer Bale where you saye that god wonderfully hath delivered you we Christiens would that you did understande that we take your deliverance from perils of your enemyes to be lyke as the common barratours doe stande by the highe waye syde to take and rob the true manne of hys goodes and after doth flee from towne to towne to save themselves. So doe we well understande you to be a notable heretike a postota and runagate whereby you are compelled of necessite to runne with the thefe or murtherer from Citie to Citie and from contrie to contrie for the assuraunce of your lyfe, but ondoutedly If you had been as you saye a true disciple of Christ and as felow lyke with Sainct Paule as you wryght your self to be, when you by chaunce of wether were dryven into Dover rode woulde lyke as Paule did as Philippus have set youre fote on lande and preached Criste but contrary wyse as you have wrytten in the fortieth lefe of your boke and on the lefte syde you were more desirous to sette youre hande to a bill of fyfty poundes more then you were able to pay to that ende you myghte be set on lande in flaunders, for that ye might have spedye travayle to the rest of your viperous brethren in Germany, wheras ye saye you wer receaved with as muche rejoyce of your myraculus deliveraunce (as you terme it) as was sainct Paule at Apiphorum of the Catholycke and christen brethren, thus this mad frantike fryer Bale in the myddest of his proude bostinges, and praisinge him selfe, dothe saye. If Helias, that wether driven runnagate remayne nowe in a foren lande, I pray thee gentyll reader marke here, how he hitteth here the nayle on the head, and of a false lying frier is becom in this one point a true tale teller, naming him selfe, Helias, with this addiscion, that wether driven runnagates, so hathe he brought hymselfe from the fellowship of saint Paule to be as he is, a runnagate, and fellowe with the unplacable enemies of Christes Churche, and companion with Cerinthus the enemye of trueth. And in the conclusyon of hys Booke the forty-fourth leafe and on the lefte syde also, he hathe divers comparysones, betwene the prophetes, apostles, and the Churche of Englande, and these are hys woordes. What shall I say more? John Baptist is nowe derided in the prison, and Jesus the sonne of God is grenned at upon the crosse, but contrarye wyse in Englande, mayster Bale, John baptist is now delivered forth of pryson. And Jesus the sonne of god is truely worshipped upon the crosse, and moreouer he sayeth: Paule in Athens is hissed at, the poore apostles are slyly laughed to scorne. But nowe in Englande praised be our lord Jesus Christ, Paule is truely preached, and the Apostles receave theyr dew honoure, and last of al he saith, John the sonne of zebede is sent into Pathinos, whiles Cerinthus, Menander, and Hebion play the heretikes at home. But otherwise I say, John zebed is now receaved forth of Pathinos in to England, and Cerinthus, Menander and Hebyon, who triumphed in Englande while John was in Pathinos, are now fledde in to Germany to play the prophets of heretikes there. The reste of Bales tr[e]achery I will omit at this time and returne to my matter.

Glossary

[(*) indicates further information in Explanatory Notes.]

abhominacions — shameful practices 309
abrenounceth — repudiates 2215
adminystracyon — giving, offering 295*
admonished — informed 1511
allegories — figures, representations 497
apayde — rewarded 74
apertly — openly, publicly 300

bawme (v) — anoint 1879
baylyfe — local magistrate or justice 1423
beckynges — bowings, noddings 672*
† bludderinge — talking nonsense 1756
bodyly — material 12
brechelesse — without breeches 1071*
brockish — beastly, dirty 1303*
by and by — immediately 623

carefull — troubled 1784
colligyners — members of a college 1291*
colour (n) — pretence 1539 (v) disguise 1170
coltish — lustful, wanton 1798
commissarye — bishop's official representative 686
commocioner — one who stirs up tumult 2125
conveyaunce — jugglery, cunning (OED 11b) 713, 1239

costomers, customer	customs official(s) 1510, 2315
crisyms	sacramental anointing 1478
croser	bishop's staff 958
crostes	crusts 84
curiouse	careful, minute 135
currishely	meanly 184
declare	make clear 249*
deprehended	detected 1042
derogacion	detraction, detriment 1004
diffarred, differred	put off, delay 1259, 1265
disparsed	sent abroad 452
doctor	teacher, instructor 38
doinge	affair, business 1181
draught	privy 388*
dyscretely	prudently 48
dyspycyons	parts of an argument (OED disposition c) 190
† effectually	explicitly 1973*
egerly	violently, severely (OED eagerly 1a) 757
Epicure	sensualist 231, irreligious 714
† Epicurysh	sensual 668
errande	notorious 1968
familiar	household 1061
fatche	fetch 398*
forced	clipped, shaven 350*
for whie	because 1888
frowardnesse	perversity 1989*
† fustene fumes	display of anger 1249
gaddinge	rushing about 558*
† gaglinge	chattering 558
galloglasses	soldiers using poleaxes 132*
Gentilite	area inhabited by non-Jewish peoples 436*
ghostly	spiritually 818
habundeth	abounds 912
hande, at no	on any account (OED 25g) 849
hande, out of	immediately 1344–45
havock	pillage, destruction 490
haynous	wicked 203
heady	overbearing (OED 1b) 331
hobby	pony 1318*
holy waterstocke	basin for holy water 1099
hospitalles	places for lodging travellers 227
howseled	given communion 2145
howsellar	priest 1481*

humayne	human, of man as distinct from God 240
in case	provided that 1350
inconveniences	offences 1288
instauntly	urgently 722
interpellacyon	appeal 1319
intreated	treated 181
jeopardyes	perils 138
justiciaryes	judges in superior courts 1015
kearnes	light armed foot soldiers 132
knowledge (v)	acknowledge 94
laboriouse	toilsome 45
† laye . . . fast (v)	fetter 1555*
layser	leisure 1024
lazar	leper 1823
lewde	unprincipled 1197
liefe tenaunt	deputy 147
loades man	pilot 1357
loose	lose 817
lubber	layabout 1460*
lurkynge	affording concealment 1150
lyddernes	rascals 75*
lyvely	vivid 23
male	travelling bag 1580
maskynge	performing 884*
meanie	collection (OED meinie 7) 113
mede	bribery 97
mere	sole, without help 96*
ministerys	trades 330
misordre	cause for confusion 1632
misterie	religious truth 410
mocion	inward prompting (OED motion sb. 9) 96
monkery	in the state of being a monk 499*
† nusled	educated (OED nuzzle v² 2δ) 547
overseane	drunk (OED overseen 1b) 1585
pageauntes	tricks 972*
palpable	can be felt 561*
parell	peril 129
parelouse	perilous 56*
† patefaction	revelation 2036
peculiar	special 344*
peltinge	worthless 1789
peltryes	rubbish (OED sb²) 200*

† Persicall   ? Persian (not in OED) 557
personage   rector's house 602
pilde   with head shaven 1789
plye   attend to 1849
point, at a   settled, decided 1642–43*
pranked   dressed up 116
pratinge   boasting 1595
prebendaryes   canons receiving prebends (incomes) 981
† priapustick   lewd, licentious 1874*
primatyve   earliest and purest (OED 1) 57
profession   vow of celibacy as a priest 693
proponed   set forth 267, 730
proselite   convert 1305
proved   tested 31
proxyes   annual payments 716
pyckarde   river or coastal sailing boat 1339
† pygion   young woman 1796*
† pylyoned   wearing a pillion, priest's or doctor's cap 350*

ravine (v)   force 1933
receptacles   places of refuge 235*
rehearsal   account 73
rejoyce (n)   cause for joy 71
resorted   came 1033
roavinge   pursuit of piracy 1536
rott   rote, heart 1311
runnegate   fugitive, wanderer 218, 1470
† rushelinge   rushing 1645

sattle   settle 1394, 1741
savegarde   safety, rescue 172*
scysmes   dissensions 1526
searcher   customs official 1374
serviceable   amenable 688
shyppers   seamen 191
skille (v)   understand 1248
slendre   unconvincing (OED 6a) 1080
sophisticall   given to false reasoning 541*
sort   number, collection 136, 1702
† spialte   ? spies (not in OED) 1797
spisinge   spicing, seasoning 1877
spret   spirit 353
staie   support (OED v² 1) 2046
stayes   supports 994
stingars   instigators with sharp tongues 525
stought   strong, robust, resolute 330, 1601
stoughtly   arrogantly 931

subscribed	signed 627
suffrages	intercessions, especially for the dead 1035*
suffren	? suffragan, assistant bishop 159, sovereign 1031
tenure	substance 654
termagaunt	blusterer, bully 1419
terrestre	earthly 29
tippeted	wearing a tippet 1796
towarde	imminent 1288
† traded with	made [my] custom 767
trayne	device, trick 940
turmoilinges	commotions 1616
† unplacable	unappeasable 2026
unsaverly	insipidly, without enthusiasm 751
unshamefast	immodest 813
untowardnesse	perversity 123
visitacion	divine intervention 1786*
vycar	representative, substitute 79*
wawled	wailed like a baby or a cat 674
wayteth upon	protects 16
ydiotes	simple and uneducated men 332

Index of Biblical Texts

When Bale writes "saith he," "saith the Lord," "saith St. Paul," and the like, he translates a Vulgate text. Sometimes his translations are rough, possibly indicating reliance upon memory. Paraphrases, unglossed references, and general references to extended passages are marked parenthetically. Psalm citations follow the numbering of the Vulgate Bible.

Old Testament

Sergio Rossi, University of Milan

Germaine Warkentin, Center for Reformation and Renaissance Studies, Victoria College, University of Toronto

Henry Woudhuysen, University College, University of London

EDITORIAL COMMITTEE for *The Vocacyon of Johan Bale*
    Gordon Kipling
    Richard S. M. Hirsch
    Arthur F. Kinney, Chair

The Renaissance English Text Society was founded to publish scarce literary texts, chiefly nondramatic, of the period 1475–1660. Originally during each subscription period two single volumes, or one double volume, were distributed to members. Beginning in 1989, with the publication of Series VII, members are billed $25 annual dues.

Subscriptions should be sent to Mario Di Cesare, Department of English, SUNY, P.O. Box 6000, Binghamton, NY 13902–6000, USA. Institutional members are requested to provide, at the time of enrollment, any order numbers or other information required for their billing records; the Society cannot provide multiple invoices or other complex forms for their needs.

Copies of publications through the 1987 volume (XII) still in print may be purchased from Associated University Presses, 440 Forsgate Drive, Cranbury, NJ 08512, USA. Beginning with volume XIII, copies will be available from MRTS — LNG-99, SUNY, P.O. Box 6000, Binghamton, NY 13902–6000.

FIRST SERIES

Vol. I. *Merie Tales of the Mad Men of Gotam* by A. B., edited by Stanley J. Kahrl, and *The History of Tom Thumbe,* by R. I., edited by Curt F. Buhler, 1965.

Vol. II. Thomas Watson's Latin *Amyntas,* edited by Walter F. Staton, Jr., and Abraham Fraunce's translation *The Lamentations of Amyntas,* edited by Franklin M. Dickey, 1967.

SECOND SERIES

Vol. III. *The dyaloge called Funus*, A Translation of Erasmus's Colloquy (1534), & *A very pleasaunt & fruitful Diologe called The Epicure*, Gerrard's Translation of Erasmus's Colloquy (1545), edited by Robert R. Allen, 1969.

Vol. IV. *Leicester's Ghost* by Thomas Rogers, edited by Franklin B. Williams, Jr., 1972.

THIRD SERIES

Vols. V-VI. *A Collection of Emblemes, Ancient and Moderne*, by George Wither, with introduction by Rosemary Freeman and bibliographical notes by Charles S. Hensley, 1975.

FOURTH SERIES

Vols. VII-VIII. *Tom a Lincolne* by R. I., edited by Richard S. M. Hirsch, 1978.

FIFTH SERIES

Vol. IX. *Metrical Visions* by George Cavendish, edited by A. S. G. Edwards, 1980.

SIXTH SERIES

Vol. X. *Two Early Renaissance Bird Poems*, edited by Malcolm Andrew, 1984.

Vol. XI. *Argalus and Parthenia* by Francis Quarles, edited by David Freeman, 1986.

Vol. XII. Cicero's *De Officiis*, trans. Nicholas Grimald, edited by Gerald O'Gorman, 1987.

Vol. XIII. *The Silkewormes and their Flies* by Thomas Moffet (1599), edited with introduction and commentary by Victor Houliston, 1988.

SEVENTH SERIES

VOL. XIV. *The Vocacyon of Johan Bale*, edited by Peter Happé and John N. King, 1989.

The Vocacyon of Johan Bale is the first edition since 1553 of John Bale's autobiographical account of his appointment in that year as Bishop of Ossory in Ireland, his conduct as a vigorous Protestant among a Catholic population, his persecution and escape, and his voyage to Holland. Bale's work is both a remarkable early piece of autobiography and an authentic portrait of the times.

Included in this volume, in addition to the original-spelling text, are an account of the text and its printing and an account of Bale's life and works and of his religious position and doctrine. The explanatory notes give a great deal of new information about Bale and those associated with him, and cross reference to his other works, especially the *Catalogus*.

Peter Happé is Principal at Barton Peveril College. His many publications include *Tudor Interludes* (1972), *English Mystery Plays* (1975), *Medieval English Drama* (1984), *The Complete Plays of John Bale* (1985–86), and numerous articles in such journals as *Medieval English Theatre* and *Renaissance Drama Newsletter.*

John N. King, Professor of English at Ohio State University, is the author of *English Reformation Literature: The Tudor Origins of the Protestant Tradition* (1986), *Tudor Royal Iconography: Literature and Art in an Age of Religious Crisis* (1989), and *Spenser's Poetry and the Reformation Tradition* (forthcoming from Princeton Univ. Press), as well as articles in journals such as *Huntington Library Quarterly, Renaissance Quarterly,* and *Yearbook of English Studies.*

mRts

medieval & Renaissance texts & studies
is the publishing program of the
Center for Medieval and Early Renaissance Studies
at the State University of New York at Binghamton.

mRts emphasizes books that are needed —
texts, translations, and major research tools.

mRts aims to publish the highest quality scholarship
in attractive and durable format at modest cost.